HOW TO WIN AN ELECTION

To Herbert Gargrave

How To Win an Election

THE COMPLETE PRACTICAL GUIDE TO
ORGANIZING AND WINNING
ANY ELECTION CAMPAIGN

ANTHONY GARGRAVE &
RAYMOND HULL

MACMILLAN OF CANADA / TORONTO

Canadian Cataloguing in Publication Data

Gargrave, Anthony, 1926-
  How to win an election
Bibliography: p.
ISBN 0-7705-1658-0 bd.   ISBN 0-7705-1671-8 pa.
1. Elections—Canada. I. Hull, Raymond, 1919-
II. Title.
JL193.G37   324'.71   C79-094214-3

The Macmillan Company of Canada Limited
70 Bond Street
Toronto, Ontario
M5B 1X3

Contents

Acknowledgments vi

Foreword vii

1 Basic Organization 1

2 Define Policy 15

3 Pick Your Candidate 29

4 Your Campaign Plan 44

5 Getting Started 60

6 The Candidate and the Public 69

7 Public Meetings 84

8 Campaign Literature 99

9 The News Media 116

10 Political Surveys 135

11 Getting Out the Vote 148

12 Raising Money 158

13 Election Day 180

14 After the Election 195

15 Elections in Associations and Clubs 203

Appendix: Candidate's Diary 217

Bibliography 225

Acknowledgments

My thanks go to Phil Lyons, President, and the other officers of the New Democratic Party, Vancouver Area Council, for giving me permission to include material circulated at a 1973 Vancouver Area Council campaign school. Some of the checklists at the end of the chapters come from that material.

Where I have drawn on material from existing literature, I have credited the authors in the text. A full bibliography is listed at the end of the book.

Many of the examples in this book are from British Columbia or the United States, but they illustrate universal principles acted on wherever people are gathered in political groups.

I would like to thank Nora Yeung for managing the manuscript, Cliff Scotten and Joel Altman for their advice, and Fred Hill for introducing me to Raymond Hull.

Foreword

When I ran in 1970 for the office of mayor in the city of Vancouver, British Columbia, I was frightened by the number of people I met during the campaign who had lost faith in the political system. They were hostile: they hated those who were active in the public life of Canada. They were bitter: they believed that the system would not work, or would not work for them. I was frightened, too, because many of them would not listen to reason. Take a large number of such alienated people, add a demagogue, and you have a dangerous situation. It was the time of the flower children and of rioting and arson in North American cities.

That is why I decided to write this book. I want to offer, to a variety of readers, an inside look at the democratic electoral system—to show how it works, and how ordinary people can make it work.

I am going to explain how to conduct a responsible and effective campaign within the democratic parliamentary system. I am not going to advocate any political programs or policies: usually, in an election, those things are decided by the groups that nominate the candidates. Neither am I going to propose any individuals as candidates: the nomination of candidates is a task for you, the Canadian voter.

I will deal with the necessity to project policy, to project the personality of the candidate, and to dramatize issues so as to reach the individual voter in the crowd.

About half the electoral constituencies in Canada could be won by almost any established party that presents its policy well, through the right candidate —one who is able to attract around himself a large enough group of dedicated, well-instructed volunteers.

Many elections are decided by only a 3-percent swing in the total vote; that is not really very much of a political change. Those small swings elect and defeat governments. Suppose, for example, that you have a provincial constituency where, at the last election,

> Jones got 37 percent of the vote,
> Smith got 33 percent of the vote,
> Brown got 30 percent of the vote.

At the next election, a 3-percent swing from Jones to Smith will defeat Jones and elect Smith. A 5-percent swing from Brown to Smith would also make Smith the winner.

Real-life election results are not quite that simple; but this illustrates how informed campaigns can create small shifts and produce political change.

I have written this book, too, because I thought that some of the Canadians who participate in politics only by voting at election-time would like to know how the system works.

Not many people want to be actors, or northern fur-traders, but a lot of people like to read how a film is made—all about scripts, lights, cameras, and makeup—or how a fur-trader carries on his business—all about traps, sleds, dogs, muskrats, beavers, and rum. It is fun to get a look behind the scenes; so, even if you do not want to be an alderman, a member of a provincial legislature, or a member of Parliament, you can read this book with interest.

Soon after an election is announced, there is a faint feeling of hysteria noticeable among the people who are involved in the battle. I get the impression that it is the same feeling that a gambler gets just after he has placed a large bet on an outside horse at the race track. This mixture of elation and anxiety is intoxicating, so be careful how you get involved. Politics is a deadly game.

When I represented the provincial riding of Mackenzie in the British Columbia legislature, I was enjoying an exciting privilege. The riding was named after Alexander Mackenzie, the explorer, and had three hundred miles of formidable, beautiful coastline and some of the finest people in the world, my constituents. They had already returned my brother, Herbert Gargrave, to the legislature twice. They returned me five times, and defeated me on my sixth try. It was a great experience, and I am grateful. All that I learned, I am going to pass on in this book.

I think it is the duty of Canadian citizens to join the political party of their choice, to help finance their party, and to work for it. You can best influence national, provincial, and urban affairs by joining with your neighbours to make your views felt. If this book makes you want to be an alderman, an MLA, or an MP, good luck. It is fun to win, or to help someone else win; and it is a bittersweet experience to lose. The system does work if you understand it. You can make it work. This book contains fifteen chapters that are fifteen levers to power. I invite you to pull those levers. If you decline the invitation, keep in mind that others will pull those levers on your behalf.

The strategy and tactics that I have presented in this book are applicable, with suitable modifications, everywhere that elections are held. While I have included a special chapter on the way to organize and run a campaign for office in community organizations and clubs, the reader will be able to pick up a great deal of useful information from the rest of the book and apply it to his own particular situation.

It was April 1952 when the phone rang in my apartment in South Vancouver, British Columbia. It was about noon, and I had just got up. In those days I worked the night shift at Eburne Sawmills. On the

other end of the line was Jessie Mendels, the
provincial secretary of the New Democratic Party, as
it is now called. "Tony," she said, "Jack Stigings of
Powell River has just phoned, and they want you to
stand for nomination as a candidate in the June
provincial election. Can you go up to Powell River
next week?"

As I held the telephone receiver to my ear, I
thought what a magnificent break I was getting.
Running for the legislature was something that I had
always wanted to do. I was only twenty-five years of
age, and I was excited at the opportunity.

"Yes," I said, "I could go up to Powell River next
week. In fact, I will be on leave of absence from the
sawmill to enable me to do some work in the interior
for the Canadian Congress of Labour; but I could be
excused from that."

Three days later I was on the way north from
Vancouver on the S.S. *Princess Mary*, a Canadian
Pacific Railway steamer that went up from Vancouver
to Powell River three times a week, arriving at Powell
River in the early evening. The steamer was late. It
was dark when I arrived, and Jack Stigings met me at
the top of the long hill from the dock.

My brother, Herbert Gargrave, had represented the
Mackenzie riding from 1941 to 1949, and the Powell
River members wanted to utilize the family name and
nominate me. I was opposed at the nominating
convention by my friend, now my colleague, lawyer
Frank Mackenzie. When the ballots were counted I
was the nominee for the 1952 provincial election. The
election was to see the old Coalition government
crushed and the minority Social Credit government
installed in British Columbia, with W. A. C. Bennett
as Premier. But at the time of my nomination nobody
knew that the old Coalition government was ready for
collapse.

After my nomination, I immediately went to see my
brother Bert to get his advice. He said, "Don't worry,
kid. You won't make it." But he offered me a cheque
for two hundred dollars for my election expenses. I

had come to stay in my brother's home at the age of
fourteen, and he had been a father to me. He had
been a member of the British Columbia legislature,
and I also wanted the excitement of the political
arena. I got it, for I won the race.

Because sophisticated polling had not yet hit
politics, and because of the weird 1952 single transferable ballot, it was almost impossible to predict
the outcome of that election. The single transferable
ballot was supposed to allow Liberals and Conser-
vatives to vote for each other on their second
vote, but as they hated each other's guts in those days
they voted secondly for either the New Democratic
Party or the Social Credit.

I was young, but I thought I was ready for it. I
had been the campaign manager in 1949 for the
Vancouver-Quadra riding when Howard Green, MP,
was returned to Ottawa, and at the same time I had
been the assistant campaign manager for the new
Vancouver South riding where my friend Grace
MacInnis, MP, was defeated in her initial run against
Arthur Laing, MP. I had also been active in the party
and on radio station CJOR's "Town Meeting".

Campaigning was fun. We hired a fishing boat and
I went all the way north from Powell River to Namu,
Bella Coola, and Ocean Falls. We stopped at every
fishing village and logging camp, put up our posters,
gave out our leaflets, and shook every hand in sight.
We also drank a lot of beer. People who live in those
communities along the coast of British Columbia
enjoy visitors, and they really do not care what your
political views are, providing you can hold up your
end of the conversation.

Finally they made up their minds and voted. I made
it, spent fourteen years in the provincial legislature,
and later fought two municipal elections in
Vancouver. And though I am now quietly practising
law in downtown Vancouver, I still look back on
those years, and my wonderful constituents, with
affection.

Basic Organization

ON YOUR MARK! GET SET!

To win an election, you cannot afford to wait until the election is called. Election-winning must be a continuous process. Then, for a few weeks before polling day, there is a time of special activity— posters, circular letters, slogans, TV debates, public meetings, and so on. This campaign is all that outsiders will see of your organization; fairly or unfairly, it represents you to the people in the street and decides whether they will vote for you or not.

In later chapters I'll discuss the less conspicuous activities that should be systematically carried on between election campaigns. But for our purpose a convenient place to begin is with the calling of an election by the head of government.

PRELIMINARY DECISIONS — Now you know when the election is coming; so the executive of your constituency, riding, or town must promptly set up the framework of the campaign.

1. Set the general theme of the campaign, and appoint a policy committee (see Chapter 2).
2. Pick a candidate; a very important choice (see Chapter 3).
3. Set the campaign budget, and plan to raise the money (see Chapter 12).
4. Appoint a campaign manager.
5. Appoint a campaign committee with general authority to wage the campaign.

6. Define any extra-special issues on which the executive must be consulted during the campaign: e.g., enlarging the campaign budget; withdrawing from the election; nominating a new candidate if the first nominee dies or withdraws.

THE CAMPAIGN MANAGER

In some places this official has the title of Campaign Chairman; but since the campaign committee also includes four or five other chairmen, I am using the title Manager, to avoid confusion.

This campaign manager must be able to organize and instruct the various officers of the campaign committee in their duties. He co-ordinates the various subcommittees, and ensures that everyone is carrying out the task assigned to him.

Normally the campaign manager prepares the agenda for all campaign committee meetings and takes the chair at those meetings. Between meetings of the campaign committee, he has the final say on all matters related to the campaign; so this must be someone with plenty of tact, and, whether he is paid or unpaid, he must be able to work full-time.

In a federal election, you will have only about 60 days' notice between the calling of the election and polling day. In a provincial election, where the province has a permanent voters' list, you may get only 38 days' notice. So I would emphasize that the campaign manager's job is a full-time job: he can then be free to work on any areas of the campaign where extra time or energy is needed.

His authority should be defined by the executive in a resolution something like this: "That Joe Smith be appointed campaign manager for this constituency, and be instructed and authorized to conduct the campaign in consultation with the candidate, as the campaign committee directs."

If you have the right person available, you may wish to appoint some dignified elder statesman as campaign chairman, part-time, while the campaign manager does the actual managing.

THE CAMPAIGN
COMMITTEE
For your campaign, you must get the widest possible participation of the people in the community; yet you cannot afford to have each of those helpers "doing his own thing". So, just as every company needs a board of directors, and every union an executive, your campaign needs a campaign committee.

I would say that about 15 members are enough for the campaign committee in an average-sized Canadian constituency. There are several ways of choosing them. For example:

1. The constituency executive might constitute itself as the campaign committee, with the president of the constituency as campaign manager.

2. The constituency executive might appoint an entirely different group of people as campaign committee and campaign manager.

3. The executive might appoint a number from their own committee as well as some other people to form the campaign committee.

Each member of the campaign committee is chosen by the elected executive, in consultation with the campaign manager, for his ability to fill a particular function. Good choices here are vital for they will be major factors in a successful campaign. There is not time to be running back to the executive, except on very important issues such as those previously mentioned; so this campaign committee has to operate quickly, efficiently, and autonomously, right through the campaign. Afterwards, it will be dissolved by the elected executive.

Here is a typical appointment resolution for a constituency executive:

That the following Campaign Committee be appointed to the respective positions alongside their names, with full authority to conduct the campaign; with the proviso that the Committee adhere to policy prescribed by the national convention and keep within the budget approved by this Executive; and further that no expenses within the budget be approved, or cheques written above $100.00, without approval in writing by the Finance Chairman; and that any expenditures made or cheques written outside the budget, and without this approval in writing, shall be the personal responsibility of the person authorizing the expenditure.

  1. Campaign Manager   (Name) _____
  2. Assistant Campaign Manager   _____
  3. Candidate   _____
  4. Candidate's Personal Representative   _____
  5. Treasurer   _____
  6. Finance Chairman   _____
  7. Headquarters Hall Manager   _____
  8. Press Officer   _____
  9. Poll Organizer and Canvass Committee Chairman_____
10. Manager of Photography   _____
11. Election-Day Manager   _____
12. Literature Chairman   _____
13. Editor of Speakers' Notes   _____
14. Transportation Chairman   _____
15. Sign Chairman   _____

1. CAMPAIGN MANAGER.   I have already described the campaign manager's duties, so let us look in some detail at the functions of the other members of the campaign committee.

2. ASSISTANT CAMPAIGN MANAGER.   He looks after details, so as to free the campaign manager for thinking, consulting with the candidate, and other important tasks. For example, the assistant manager should keep copies of all basic documents in a safe place, separate from campaign headquarters; then, in case of fire or theft, you are prepared to start up again.

3. CANDIDATE.   He is before the public much of the time throughout the campaign, canvassing, main-streeting, or speaking at meetings. He should also be around the committee rooms or campaign head-quarters in time to meet canvassers as they return from an evening's canvassing. He will encourage the

canvassers and listen carefully to what they are learning on the doorstep. The candidate should not be involved with the budget or the campaign funds, except for personal, out-of-pocket expenses.

4. CANDIDATE'S PERSONAL REPRESENTATIVE. Obviously, this should be someone who gets on well with the candidate; indeed, the candidate usually selects him. This personal representative takes the load of routine activities off the candidate, and leaves him, as far as possible, free for active campaigning. The representative can also conveniently serve as official agent.

5. TREASURER. He is responsible for receiving, paying out, and keeping track of all money during the campaign. He will have to account for every cent when the hoopla of the elections has died away. You must be strict about that.

6. FINANCE CHAIRMAN. As head of the finance committee, he is responsible for preparing the budget for approval by the executive, and for *raising* the campaign funds. He must also approve all major expenditures.

7. HEADQUARTERS HALL MANAGER. He looks after the headquarters hall, maintains the files, makes election material available to the public, and organizes teams of workers to answer phones or do clerical work. He is also responsible for security of the hall: you do not want to lose valuable records by fire or theft the day before the election.

8. PRESS OFFICER. This member, if possible, should be a professional journalist or newsman. He is responsible for paid advertisements, press releases, and all other news announcements. He should compile a list of contacts in each of the media who can assure that your releases receive attention. The publicity committee, under his direction, will see to preparing

the campaign leaflets. In a situation like a civic election, where there are several candidates, the candidates may do rough drafts of their own releases, but it is helpful if the press officer, or someone else from the publicity committee, does a final draft before they are released.

9. POLL ORGANIZER AND CANVASS COMMITTEE CHAIRMAN. This is a full-time job. He is responsible for the systematic and repeated canvass of all polls. He must ensure that all canvassers complete their work on time and that records of canvassing are kept and protected.

10. MANAGER OF PHOTOGRAPHY. He arranges to provide copies of the usual head-and-shoulders photos of the candidate, plus several informal shots, such as candidate in shirtsleeves and candidate kissing spouse. The manager should also keep a photographic record of the campaign from the start. If you lose, you probably won't be able to bear the sight of the pictures, but if you win, you will love them.

11. ELECTION-DAY MANAGER. He gets the longest time of all the committee members to prepare for his task—one or two months. Then, at 5 a.m. on election day, he takes complete command. He must see that each inside scrutineer is in place at the poll, that each outside worker or runner is assigned to his post, and that each proven supporter votes. He should advise his troops to eat a hearty breakfast, and to bring their own lunches. When the polls close, he must see that the final count is prompt and accurate. At about 10 p.m. on election day, his job is finished.

12. LITERATURE CHAIRMAN. He stocks and cares for copies of the basic leaflets and basic poster, and also for specialized literature for concerned citizens. He does various other jobs, as he is instructed during the campaign. He may operate a duplicating machine to churn out meeting announcements or statements on emergent local issues.

13. EDITOR OF SPEAKERS' NOTES.   He drafts material for 30-second, 1-minute, and 5-minute radio and TV spots, and also writes notes for longer speeches—those up to 30 minutes. A well-prepared speakers' manual gives direction and focus to the whole campaign. It helps to improve the performance of new candidates and other less-qualified speakers. Details of this project are given in Chapter 5.

14. TRANSPORTATION CHAIRMAN.   He provides automobiles and drivers for the candidate, and for any of the campaign committee who need them. Until election day, 1 or 2 passenger cars and 1 truck are usually enough; but on election day he must produce a fleet of automobiles and volunteer drivers to get all identified supporters to vote. Many people enjoy helping with this work: some will just lend a car; others will volunteer to drive. It's an important job, because a voter who turns up five minutes after the poll has closed is no help to your campaign; nor is the voter who says, the day after the election, "If only I'd known the result was going to be so close, I would have voted." A good transportation chairman gets these people to the poll. It may mean the difference between victory and defeat.

15. SIGN CHAIRMAN.   He must find locations for his big plywood signs, manufacture and paint them, erect them on front lawns, and recover them on the day after the election. It can be a demanding job. He needs about a dozen strong helpers and a half-ton pickup truck.

   No campaign committee member should be left to work alone: the whole committee should be kept informed of the progress of all aspects of the campaign. The campaign manager should be in touch with each committee head daily: the full campaign committee should meet at least twice a week, to review progress, to discover any weak spots in the campaign, and to make any necessary decisions. To facilitate this, meetings should take place late in the evening, or very early in the morning, when people cannot be out canvassing or doing other work that involves the public. Then all members will be able to attend. You may wish to publish a campaign news bulletin, a sort of gossip sheet for those in the know.

CAMPAIGN HEADQUARTERS
As early as possible, choose your campaign headquarters. Here are some hints:

1. You need not pay high rent for a supposedly "good" address, but you should look for a place on a busy street: the more pedestrian and vehicular traffic passing, the better. Thus the headquarters serves not only as an office, but as an advertisement.

2. Premises all at basement or upper-floor level are not good; at least a part should be on street level (e.g., a storefront or a public hall leased for the duration). Abandoned churches or hotels are excellent.

3. To deal with the public, you need office or reception space near the street, preferably with big windows.

4. You need ample work space where your officers and supporters can hold meetings, keep records, produce signs, and print and store publicity material. There should also be a private office for the campaign manager.

5. Ample parking space is useful.

These are ideal conditions. You may not be able to fulfil them all, but get the best you can. The campaign headquarters is not only a centre of activity for your supporters, it should be a centre *from which* activity is flowing out to the constituency. So the right location can make a big difference to your campaign. If you are leasing premises, get a lease in writing, even if it is only written on the back of an envelope, pay the rent, and obtain a receipt for it.

EQUIPMENT
Get 2 or 3 telephones, one of them in the campaign manager's office. See that the numbers are correctly listed on your literature. If you are going to canvass by phone, you will need up to 20

phones. You will find the telephone company ready to give prompt, careful service.

Prominent on the wall of the headquarters should be an organizational chart of the campaign committee. Here everybody can check his own duties, and see who to ask about anything else. Beside each name, put the person's address and phone number, with alternate phone numbers where available.

Get typewriters, desks, file cabinets, tables, according to the space available and the number of your workers. Do not skimp on this equipment: you need enough so that everyone who volunteers can be given some useful task. This air of productive activity and efficiency is valuable in maintaining enthusiasm.

Ample facilities for light refreshments are useful. You do not want campaign workers continually drifting away to coffee shops and bars. All of them should be able to get together in the headquarters over coffee and snacks, to exchange experiences and chat with the candidate.

OTHER OFFICE SPACE   It would, no doubt, be simplest for the candidate and the campaign manager if the whole campaign could be run from the kind of headquarters I have just described. That would be the easiest place to hold all the meetings, formal and informal, and to make all the myriad decisions that keep a campaign moving. Some compact big-city constituencies may be able to operate like that, but many places will need a number of satellite campaign offices, or "committee rooms" as they are often called. Here are some reasons for opening such committee rooms and a few hints on operating them.

1. SIZE OF CONSTITUENCY.   In my own provincial Mackenzie riding, for example, transportation was slow, difficult, and expensive; it took a campaign manager a day to travel from one district to another! Such big rural constituencies would probably have to be divided, for organizational purposes, into several regions, each with some unifying economic or social

interest, or marked off by some geographical feature. Each region would have its own local campaign manager, and would raise its own funds. The unifying forces would be the candidate, a basic campaign leaflet, and a basic poster.

Some thinly populated rural areas may need one committee room for each poll—perhaps someone's basement or front porch. In such districts, where everyone knows everyone else, these local committee rooms can be very effective.

2. SPECIAL AREAS. Even in a compact constituency, certain areas may have special characteristics of their own. For effective public relations, such districts may have their own satellite committee rooms.

I remember the 1975 provincial campaign in Vancouver Centre. This time I was not a candidate: my only formal duty was to be a scrutineer on election day. A group of young Chinese people came to the campaign committee and volunteered to find, rent, and staff a committee room on Pender Street, in the middle of Vancouver's populous Chinatown. The campaign committee, delighted, told them to go ahead.

A few days later, I visited this auxiliary committee room. It was festooned with bright banners and posters in Chinese characters; there were abundant Chinese foodstuffs for campaign workers. As an old campaigner, I felt pleased to see these young enthusiasts so busily conducting an election in their own area. We won that constituency.

3. THE NEIGHBOURHOOD STRATEGY. You can fight an election mainly through street-level committee rooms, scattered through your whole territory, at least one in each identifiable region. Each committee room runs its own neighbourhood campaign very much on its own terms, with no strict control from headquarters. This method could be described as "storefront" or "street-wise" campaigning.

There are risks in this degree of decentralization: you may find, or your opponents may pounce upon, some awkward clashes in the policy statements emerging from the different committee rooms. Nevertheless, in a constituency that has many ethnic neighbourhoods, with widely different characteristics, it may be the best way to go.

THE FIRST MEETING   Soon after its appointment, the campaign committee should meet. These items should be on the agenda:
1. Receive the executive resolution appointing the campaign committee.
2. Give each member written instructions, so that he knows his duties and what he must get done and how much time he has to do it. The campaign manager will have these instructions concisely drawn up in advance. Here is the kind of detail needed:
   (a) If the member has to form a committee of his own (e.g. policy, finance, publicity), how many members must it have? What is it to do and by what dates?
   (b) Date and business of first meeting. Frequency of subsequent meetings.
   (c) Date and contents of the committee chairman's first report back to the campaign manager.
3. Set up a small policy committee, which includes the candidate. (Chapter 2 gives detailed suggestions on policy formation.)
4. Set up the finance committee, to be concerned, not with budgeting or with keeping accounts, but solely with raising money. That means, essentially, *asking* people for money, eyeball to eyeball, so the committee members should be people who are dedicated to, and good at, this sensitive task.
5. Draw up a budget. Decide how much you want to spend or how much you have to spend; make up your mind to stay with that decision—not to overspend the budget, no matter what the

pressure. This budget forms part of the instructions for the finance chairman and tells him how much he must plan to raise.

6. Appoint an election historian to keep track of all literature and press releases issued, news clippings, statements by opposing candidates, and correspondence, plus names and addresses of your supporters.

7. If you do not already have an official candidate, set a date for the nominating meeting.

8. Set up an administrative committee of about 3 people—say the campaign manager, the candidate, and one other—to act between meetings of the full campaign committee.

9. Set someone looking for a campaign headquarters.

10. Set a date for the next full campaign committee meeting.

For the sake of clarity, I am describing what I think is an ideal set-up, but it may be best for your purposes to have a smaller campaign committee—say 8 members, or 5; then each member would have more than one task.

CIVIC ELECTIONS   The basic organization described above is suitable for federal or provincial elections; but in civic, municipal, regional-district, or other local elections, there must be a few differences, because of the number of candidates involved—for mayor, aldermen, parks board, or school board. In a typical Vancouver civic election, for example, each party may have up to 26 candidates running. To have all of them on your campaign committee would make it unmanageable.

In such a case, you could appoint to the campaign committee your mayoralty candidate and one each from aldermanic, school-board, and parks-board slates. Nevertheless, the three full slates of candidates—for aldermen, and parks and school boards—should meet regularly on their own—say, twice a week—to discuss strategy, share information, and arrange speaking engagements.

GETTING IT ON
PAPER

I am emphasizing the importance of *written* plans of action, instructions, and progress reports. Written directions are valuable to newcomers with no experience of campaigns; they are useful too, for experienced members who may not have done the particular jobs they are doing now. Even for the veteran campaigner, written orders and reports are useful. Maybe, through sickness or some other reason, he will have to hand over his responsibilities in mid campaign; how convenient then to have a detailed, written description of what has been done, and what remains to be done.

Written instructions also enforce responsibility and accountability. For this purpose, issue checklists for the various campaign procedures. The checklist reminds the worker, step by step, of what he has to do; it also offers a convenient way for him to report back to his committee chairman, the campaign manager, or the candidate.

Here, for example, is a checklist for setting up the campaign headquarters, or a committee room.

COMMITTEE-
ROOM
CHECKLIST

The committee room should have:
- main-street frontage with good traffic flow
- easy ground-floor access
- large windows; clear view of interior for the public on the street
- adequate artificial lighting
- space for: a small office in the back; a large area in front for clerical work, organization of canvassing, and committee meetings; a public reception area
- washroom facilities
- kitchen facilities
- parking space
- at least 4 electrical outlets
- a cooler for soft drinks
- 3 typewriters
- duplicating machine—preferably a simple offset-printing machine
- 3 phones
- a number of desks and file cabinets

- 30 chairs and 3 large tables made of heavy plywood and sawhorses
- pens, pencils, and erasers
- stationery
- copies of the *Elections Act* and *Instructions for Returning Officers and Candidates*
- maps of the constituency, coloured to show strong points
- list of registered voters and a list of poll locations
- names, addresses, and phone numbers of candidate and committee
- mailing lists of constituency members and other groups of people in the riding, such as union members, doctors, clergymen, etc.
- forms to be completed by citizens volunteering to help
- chart of workers, showing poll and function assigned to each
- summaries of party policy
- biographies of the candidate
- displays of literature, books, and campaign leaflets
- display in street window
- large linear plan of dates and activities, showing a timetable for the campaign
- chart showing candidate's activities: where he is speaking, with whom he is canvassing, media engagements, etc.
- wall charts showing polls being canvassed and progress on each poll
- "thermometer" or some such chart, showing progress in raising money
- charts indicating progress of election-day organizing

Define Policy

WHAT WILL YOU DO IF YOU WIN?

An election is a contest in persuasion and debate. The 4 major factors which determine the result of that contest are party loyalty, party policy, the character of the candidate, and the character of the party leader. Party loyalty has been carefully built over the years, and the party leader is often chosen in some distant city, but candidates and election programs are often chosen shortly before an election. It sometimes happens that the process of defining policy can help in the selection of the candidate, so I will deal with policy first.

THE POLICY COMMITTEE

As I mentioned in Chapter 1, you must set up a committee to form an election program for your campaign. This policy-formation is a task that calls for realism. You do not want any dreamy idealists on this committee; nor do you need the sour, cynical types who think that any policy which is popular in a democracy must of necessity be immoral. Such people think that if a doctor's prescription tastes good it cannot be effective. Those two types spell trouble on a policy committee and defeat in an election.

The policy committee needs a firm, thoughtful person as chairman; also a secretary capable of drawing up clear, concise reports of the committee's findings. When a candidate has been selected, he should become a permanent member of the policy committee.

If yours is a purely local organization, or a new party, you can start from scratch and try to evolve a policy which is acceptable to your present supporters, meets local needs, and will win you local support.

If you belong to a national or provincial party, you have less freedom. Let us see how to proceed in that case.

NATIONAL PLANKS AND LOCAL PLATFORMS

You may want to start by analysing the national or provincial policy of your party, as set at party conventions or defined by the party constitution. Has that policy lately been revised? If not, is it likely to be revised before the election?

Suppose, for example, that your national policy includes better old-age pensions, and your constituency contains an exceptionally high proportion of retired people. Here is an issue that might usefully be emphasized.

Some features of national policy may be of no particular local interest. Suppose, for example, that you have a national plank on the bank rates. In an agricultural district, farmers might be much more concerned with construction and maintenance of roads. In a small town, the decisive local issue might be parking meters.

Some national planks might positively injure your cause locally. Perhaps your national leader advocates reducing tariffs and encouraging international trade, while your constituency is suffering unemployment because of imported automobiles and television sets. From your point of view, then, the less said about tariff reduction the better. Or suppose your national policy includes high tariffs. If you are campaigning in the consumer West, there is no point in advocating such tariffs, which are designed to protect eastern industry.

THE LOCAL ELECTORATE

It would not be too difficult to draw up a policy that would appeal to a homogeneous group of like-minded people—say, all coal-miners, all automobile-factory workers, or all farmers. But you cannot expect to deal with a uniform public. You must be prepared to aim at a number of "publics", each of which sees life from a different point of view.

Here are the sorts of questions that should be asked in order for you to prepare this analysis of your constituents. What are their ethnic backgrounds? How many of them are Canadians? How many of these are citizens and registered voters? How many of the voters are United Empire Loyalists who regard their grandfathers as part of Canadian history? How many, if any, are of French descent, and what proportion of these are separatists? How many, if any, are of native Indian descent?

What proportion of your electorate is in each age group? Nineteen-year-old voters do not have the same interests as old-age pensioners. You might like the idea of appealing to the young voters; but you will often find that young people do not register to vote. It is the middle-aged homeowner who registers to vote and plods regularly to the polls at each election; so if you cannot influence that group, you are in trouble.

Who are the natural leaders in your community—civic officials, trade-union officials, business executives, clergymen, schoolteachers? How can you meet them? If too many of these recognized leaders oppose your policy, you will not stand much chance of winning the election. In the Vancouver Centre constituency, where I now live, they used to say that the most important opinion-moulders in town were the bartenders.

It is an advantage if the candidate has lived in the constituency for a long time and knows the answers to all of these questions. If he is a newcomer, he will do well to sit down with a map, poll-by-poll results of the last election, some census-tract information, and some knowledgeable members of the committee, to study the subject.

Your test for each policy idea at election time is: "How many voters will be interested in it?"

If most voters are not interested in a policy, or

cannot understand it, then that policy will not help to win the election for you. What you must prepare and offer to the local electorate is a policy that will make people want to vote for your candidate.

I am not offering an argument for electoral success at any price, but I am pointing out the difference between a political party and a school of philosophy, between a policy committee and a debating society. A political party is a machine for achieving power. If you do not gain power in a parliamentary democracy, your policy is not put into practice, and somebody else operates the machinery of government. A campaign committee should leave philosophizing to the party's annual convention.

LOCAL ECONOMIC ISSUES

In every election you will have to consider local economic issues. I will describe, for example, how this was done in my old British Columbia provincial constituency of Mackenzie. This constituency covers 300 miles of the British Columbia coast between Vancouver and Prince Rupert. The voters of Mackenzie were diversified: 10 percent native Indians, 50 percent industrial workers, and 40 percent retired people. The Indians, mostly fishermen, were evenly scattered along the coast. The factory workers lived in the pulp-and-paper towns of Ocean Falls, Powell River, Port Mellon, and Woodfibre. Most of the retired people were grouped on the Sechelt Peninsula, in the southern end of the constituency, not far from Vancouver.

The one issue that affected all the people up and down that long stretch of coastline was communications: they wanted good postal service, telephone service, water and air transportation, and good roads. In some places, such as Bella Coola and Ocean Falls, they just wanted roads of any kind.

When I held the seat, I kept pressing for cheaper freight rates, so Bella Coola farmers could get their potatoes to market. I kept advocating the formation of a Canadian coast-guard to protect the people who

used the sea for transportation, and in those days that
included just about everybody in that area.

On other matters, the various groups of Mackenzie
voters might differ, but on the one issue of transportation they were all agreed. A candidate could
not have been elected in Mackenzie if the voters had
felt that another person, or another party, would have
done a better job of obtaining those communication
facilities.

There were other issues that affected only certain
parts of that constituency. The Powell River district,
for example, had a population of about 16,000, with
one main employer, the MacMillan Bloedel Limited
paper-mill. Powell River's problems were:

1. Transportation by bus, air, road, and sea. For
this community the issue usually crystallized into an
argument over ferry rates and schedules. So what
would be a modest, practicable improvement?

2. Pollution from the mill, usually a harmless but
unpleasant smell. What would be a remedy: air-
pollution legislation, voluntary technical im-
provements by the company, or a government
grant?

3. Markets for newsprint and wood pulp. Would
the solution be technical development, more capital
investment, and a better sales force? Or would it lie in
a reduced government royalty on logs?

The southern part of the Mackenzie riding was
commonly called the Sechelt Peninsula. It included the
rural communities of Pender Harbour, Sechelt, and
Gibsons, and the industrial townsite of Port Mellon,
on Howe Sound. It held about one-third of the voters:
there were many retired people who were permanent
residents, many summer-home dwellers, and the
industrial workers at Port Mellon.

The policy which I evolved for this region was as
follows:

1. Rebuild the main highway to modern standards
or relocate it.

2. Preserve seashore public parks along the coast.

3. Promote the construction of a large, resort-type hotel at Pender Harbour. This sort of hotel could employ more people than the Port Mellon pulp mill, and a lot of those employees could be women.

4. Establish a hospital chronic wing, a rest home, and living quarters for senior citizens at Sechelt.

Thus you will have to consider what are the economic issues in your community, or in certain parts of it. In one place, construction of freeways, bridges, and tunnels might be high on the list. Do you favour such development, with all its implications—increased use of the internal-combustion engine, greater consumption of oil, and the consequent need for more vigorous oil exploration at home, or increased oil imports from abroad?

If you are not for freeways and bridges, how about urban or inter-urban rapid transit? Who wants it? Who is to pay for it? Where are the routes to go? Who could gain and who could lose by owning property close to such routes?

In coming years, economic policy will have to deal increasingly with conserving resources and with preserving the environment. This may call for such measures as water-rationing, reduction of street lighting, and economies in the heating of public buildings. Pollution control, for many people, used to mean checking the smoke from a steel mill or the effluent from a fish cannery: it may soon involve restrictions on what were once considered private activities—such things as walking your dog in the park, burning your own garbage, or barbecuing your own supper in your own backyard. Such problems will call for careful thought by your policy committee.

I do not mean to imply that there is anything very mysterious or difficult about constructing a local or regional economic plan for a constituency. Plenty of people in the locality know what needs to be done. Yet these local problems are commonly ignored by provincial and national policy-makers. The remedy? Consult those local experts; get a map of the area and a group of people who understand it. With such a foundation, your policy committee can identify the local problems, specify some solutions, and assign priorities to the objectives.

OPPOSITION
POLICY

In forming your policy, you cannot afford to overlook the policy of your opposition. In some elections, the opposition may consist of one candidate, backed by a party; another time, it might be two, three, or more candidates, each with party backing, plus an independent with no party. In some civic elections, the opposition might run to a score or more candidates, some backed by parties, others independent. So analysis of opposition policy may range from fairly simple to exceedingly complex; but in either case, you cannot afford to dodge it.

Let us look at a straightforward case: there are only two candidates; your opponent at present holds the seat and you are trying to oust him. Here are some things to consider. First, study his policy in the last election.

1. Summarize his former policy in a brief list of proposals or promises. As a basis for this study, it would be useful to have copies of his literature from the last campaign.

2. How, if at all, did it differ from the general policy of his party?

3. Which items of the previous policy, if any, did he successfully carry out?

4. Which proposals, if any, did he neglect to carry out?

5. Which items of opposition policy did you or your party oppose at the time? Have any of these items turned out badly?

Then you will need a similar analysis of your opponent's policy for the forthcoming election.

1. If he has already announced his current policy, study it. If he has not announced it, try to estimate what it will be.

2. How does his current policy differ from that of the previous election?

3. Which items of his new policy, if any, do you agree with? It can be awkward for your campaign if you find yourself in agreement with the opposition on too many points, especially if he is *in* and you are *out*. So if it looks as if that is happening—too many points of agreement—you should consider seeking more policy points on which you know the opposition will not agree with you. You have to create political distance.

4. Which items of his new policy do you oppose, and why? Have you prepared all the evidence and arguments you will need to justify that opposition?

This analysis of the opponent's policy will be urgently needed for planning your own policy, and for preparing your own speeches. It will be particularly useful if your opponent springs one of those powerful surprise items partway through the campaign. If you have been expecting it, you can counterattack immediately. It will be useful to have one or more members of the policy committee concentrate on this analysis of opposition policy and report back to the committee.

YOUR TACTICS TOWARDS THE OPPOSITION   Thorough policy analysis will provide you with some useful tactical points for dealing with the opposition. Here are a few more hints.

If your opponent is a member of some ethnic or religious minority, I would suggest that you do not comment on that fact. If your candidate is attacked because of his minority status, his best defence is to keep cool and simply reply that he intends to represent everybody in the constituency. Do not have him make an issue of his own minority status. This impartial attitude will help your candidate gain status in the eyes of the more responsible voters.

POSITIVE POLICY   Always bear in mind that you are aiming at the undecided voter. Supporters of the other party or parties are not going to vote for you in any event. Your own party faithful are already committed. So you are after those undecided voters who elect or defeat every candidate. Yes, those waverers decide who represents the constituency, so your policy must be framed to appeal to them.

In some situations, you may be able to get elected on a negative, one-plank platform: "Stop the war!", for example, or "Stop the freeway!" But as a general rule, your policy must be positive: you must be *for* something. Moreover, a positive policy helps to give cohesion to your organization—literature committee, media committee, canvassers, and candidate: it gives them something specific to work with, something definite to offer the public. The whole campaign effort is directed towards projecting the policy through the personification of the candidate and the party; that projection is best achieved with a *positive* policy.

There is an ever-recurring temptation towards variety and complexity of policy. It is a temptation that particularly besets the earnest student of politics: he sees so many wrongs to right and deficiencies to be made good, so many under-privileged people to be helped, so many schools, hospitals, and airfields to be improved. The policy committee must resist this temptation.

Of course, you should have a wide variety of ideas to work with. Encourage the conservative members of the committee to put their views forward; also encourage the most imaginative ones. Then, by patient discussion, you can proceed to discard some ideas, to combine others, to simplify, to refine, to clarify, to decide on your priorities. Committee members should find all this enjoyable: after all, politicians are in the idea business. But get these policy discussions over early in the campaign.

The eventual aim is to draw up a *concise* program. If your campaign is to have focus and be effective you should have no more than 6 basic points; a 3-point program might be better.

A concise program gives guidance to everybody in the organization; it gives you something easily comprehensible, something memorable, to present to the uncommitted voter. You will have little enough time to communicate with him, so the simpler your message, the more effective it is.

A SLOGAN   When the policy is thus defined, try to sum up the whole thing in one concise, easily remembered slogan. This slogan can then be repeated on every piece of campaign literature. It will become your "monogram", so be sure to create something you can live with. Some slogans do not wear well with the passage of time, so take care: a slogan that seems powerful for you and your party now might perhaps become an embarrassment if the opposition drags it out in mid term or at the next election.

PRELIMINARY   Even the best-informed policy committee should not
TESTING   wait for the election result to test the policy it has drawn up. Test your policy as soon as you can: this testing should certainly be completed by the early part of the campaign. Much better, of course, is a continuous process of policy formation and testing going on between campaigns, so that when an election is called, you have a complete policy ready to put forward. Here are some testing techniques.

1. The first method of testing a policy proposal would commonly be to discuss it with your political associates—people who are not on the policy committee and did not have a hand in drawing it up. You can do this formally, by speeches and debates, or informally, by conversation. This method is useful, but it is not enough by itself: people actively involved in politics are only a minority of the electorate, and because of their political activity, their opinions on public issues tend to differ from those of the average voter. It is highly desirable to find what that average voter thinks.

2. You can test a proposal by talking it over with a few people who know the neighbourhood well, who also know you well enough to be frank in their comments, and who are *not* themselves active in politics. This might include some friends and members of your family. Ask your mother-in-law what she

thinks of the proposed course of action. If, when you have finished describing it, she says "Eh?", you will have to reword it to make it understandable. Many non-politicians, you will find, do not grasp political issues so readily as do your political co-workers: that is primarily because they are not constantly talking, reading, and thinking about such matters. I remember reading a newspaper statement by a candidate in one election in which he stressed his unshakable opposition to "Schachtian economics". I doubt whether one voter in a hundred would recognize the term.

3. No less valuable is the "indirect survey". You can try this technique on casual acquaintances, fellow workers, or strangers, anywhere you get the chance. Do not come flat out and say, "I'm conducting a survey of public opinion on such-and-such a subject. What do you think about it?" Many people, when formally asked for a statement on some political subject, dry up; others often say something different from what they really think.

The "indirect survey" technique is simply to steer the conversation to the desired topic, often by a comment on some current news item concerning that subject. Keep the conversation going until you find out what the person thinks about it. Afterwards you can jot down the person's opinion on any point that concerns you; fuller notes should also be made of any specially useful comments he has made.

4. A testing technique often used by someone who is already in office is called "The Trial Balloon". Suppose a minister of the Crown has a controversial policy which he wants to introduce. He "leaks" it to a newspaperman. Out comes a story under some such headline as: Minister To Remove Milk Subsidy. Then the minister sits back and waits. After the discussion has died down, he can gauge the public acceptability of the policy. If there is a storm of protest, or if some new, unfavourable evidence emerges, the minister can say he is not going to introduce any such policy. What he has done is to consult with his constituency

which, on such an issue, might be a whole province or the whole country. If he is a sensitive, sensible minister, he will take the advice he derived from his "leak".

5. You can also take a formal, scientifically balanced survey. For details on this technique see Chapter 10.

So, with each of your new policies, ask, test, poll, *see* if you can authenticate your information. If you find that an item is well understood, but is widely disapproved of, then consider whether to discard it. If the unpopular item is a matter of principle, then keep it by all means; but do not expect it to help you win the election.

NOTHING
CERTAIN

No amount of advance testing can tell you for certain how all voters will react to a proposal, but testing is a valuable guide, and undoubtedly should be used by anyone seriously interested in drawing up a sound, election-winning policy.

IN-BETWEEN
ISSUES

I have stressed the need for careful formation of policy as early as is practicable. Yet there may arise, during the campaign, some critical issue which is not covered in the formal program—what I call an in-between issue. An in-between issue may be suddenly created by some events, unpredictable and beyond your control.

Here are some examples of in-between issues that I have been faced with during election campaigns, and the action I took.

1. There was a mudslide at Ocean Falls that caused serious damage and loss of life. *Action*: we called on the responsible minister by telegram for immediate assistance, and had a survivor of the slide, wearing a large white surgical leg cast, act as the chairman of our election meeting.

2. An opponent promised to build a road and establish a vital ferry link. *Action*: we adopted our opponent's plan for the new road and ferry crossing

as our own policy and saw it established while I was a member of the legislature. I enjoyed stealing that road and ferry plank. Do not hesitate to adopt a good idea.

3. I was accused of crossing a union picket line. *Action*: I immediately denied the accusation, which was false.

4. Someone started a rumour that the current election would be ruled invalid by the courts. *Action*: we quickly assured our supporters that the story was false, and urged them to redouble their efforts for the election.

In an emergency, the candidate alone may have to improvise some statement on an in-between issue; but a better way to solve the problem is by consultation. The candidate should be able to talk of such issues with some, or all, of the campaign committee and, if there is time, with other experienced people in the party. This is worth taking some trouble over: an in-between issue may win or lose an election.

CANDIDATES
AND POLICY   I believe that a legislative member or a candidate has two apparently conflicting roles. If elected, he is responsible for reflecting his constituents' views, as well as he can, in the legislature: but at the same time, a member or candidate has a duty to *lead* his constituents on public issues. Similarly, a lawyer or doctor is of absolutely no use if he says to his client or patient, "Well, what advice would you like today?" Indeed, parliamentary democracy will not work without confident, committed leadership—something that the voter can accept or reject. Most voters, most of the time, are not voting on single political issues, but on the questions "Who shall represent us in the legislature? Who can we trust?"

For example, I would not vote for capital punishment, no matter what my constituents thought about the subject. But if I wished to oppose capital punishment contrary to the wishes of my constituents, I would have to find out why they favoured it. And I will lay a modest wager that, if I carefully explained my position to my constituents, I could still win the election, even if a majority opposed my view on that particular issue.

By this process of explaining, leading, and reconciling, a politician can play an important role in a fanatical world.

POLICY   An effective policy-formation technique is to ask each
SEMINARS   prospective candidate to prepare a complete policy statement for delivery at a seminar; then you see how each of them performs. A little cruel, perhaps, but then so is politics.

Although there would be no time for such policy seminars during an election campaign, they could be held in those dog-days between elections. They help to form policy and to select candidates; moreover, they have considerable entertainment value.

 # Pick Your Candidate

The selection of the candidate is the most important decision your constituency will make. It deserves careful thought and careful planning. The campaign committee is going to invest thousands of dollars in the candidate once he is nominated; the hopes of a lot of loyal party members are resting on him, and his victory or defeat may affect the outcome of the election, the composition of the next government, and the future of the country.

A PERSONAL RELATIONSHIP From the first day that you launch your campaign, individual voters are making up their minds. Those voters are influenced by party loyalty and party policy; but experience confirms that they are also strongly influenced by your candidate and by the way he expounds that policy.

Can you find a candidate with a wide range of experience as well as the ability to interest people in the policy of your party or group? Can you find a candidate whose relationship with the voters becomes, for them, a significant experience? Find such a candidate, and you are well on the road to an electoral majority. It is worth looking hard. Many an election has been lost because the right candidate was never asked to run.

THE
CANDIDATE'S
COMMITTEE

The party members in each constituency choose their candidate; but in practice an important responsibility for selection is undertaken by a special candidate's committee. Then the choice or choices of that committee are confirmed or not confirmed by the full membership at a nominating convention or meeting.

While you cannot afford to delay your search until the election is announced, there is no point in starting too early. The candidate's committee should begin its search 18 months before the anticipated election.

About 5 is the right number of members for the candidate's committee, and they should represent, as far as possible, a cross-section of the community. Each member of this committee should make a written statement forgoing his right to receive the nomination, for, if one or two of the people on this committee really want the nomination themselves, you will never get a fair assessment of the other people who are available as candidates.

QUALIFICA-
TIONS OF
CANDIDATES

Section 20 of the *Canada Elections Act* states that, to qualify as a candidate, a person must first be qualified as an elector. Section 14 states that every man and woman who has attained the age of 18 on polling day and is a Canadian citizen is qualified as an elector. So it does your would-be candidate no good to have lived in Canada for fifty years if he has not got around to taking out Canadian citizenship.

But not every elector can become a candidate. Section 21 of the *Act* states that these persons are *ineligible* as candidates in a federal election:
(a) those recently convicted of election offences
(b) members of provincial legislatures or councils
(c) sheriffs or judicial officers
(d) salaried civil servants, unless granted leave
(e) the Chief Electoral Officer and his assistant
(f) returning officers
(g) judges
(h) jailed prisoners
(i) those mentally ill

(j) members of the armed forces, except reservists
(k) government contractors
    The *Provincial Elections Act* of British Columbia is
different. In a B.C. provincial election, it is *not*
sufficient to be qualified as an elector: you must also
be registered as a voter and have resided in the
province for a period of 12 months. I mention this
point as a warning to check your own statute. There
is no use wasting the committee's time investigating
people who are then found to be ineligible to run.

A MAN OR A
WOMAN

I have written so far about the candidate and *his*
policy and *his* victory, but I certainly do not mean to
imply that the candidate must be a man. Many people
responsible for selecting candidates do feel that their
candidates must be men. Look at a few elected
assemblies such as the legislature at your provincial
capital, or Parliament at Ottawa, and you will see
that in most of them, far more men than women are
being nominated and elected.

Although this situation changes from decade to
decade and from one locale to another, I would say
that, at the moment, a woman candidate has a slight
edge on a man. In the past, women voters would not
support women candidates, but now, if other things
are equal, they do. While it used to be that a woman
candidate's job was to impress the men, today she has
to impress the women, and that can be tough. This
present tendency of women to vote for women is a
new built-in advantage, brought about by the activism
of various women's groups.

In the 1974 federal election, there was a fascinating
contest for the Skeena riding that illustrates this
tendency I've been talking about. The riding
surrounds the Skeena River in northwestern British
Columbia, and includes the Pacific port of Prince
Rupert. It is a vast area with rugged terrain and a
tough climate. The loggers and fishermen who work
there require a no-nonsense approach by the
candidate; about 10 percent of the voters are native
Indians.

In 1974 Frank Howard held the seat for the New Democratic Party. We had sat together as members of the Provincial Legislature at Victoria from 1953 until 1956, when Frank had decided to enter federal politics and run for Skeena. He was a logging-truck driver and trade-union organizer, bright, good-looking, and an effective speaker. The local union endorsed him, and he had good relations with the native Indians. He could identify with his constituents and they could identify with him. The voters liked him as a candidate and liked the policy of his party, the New Democratic Party. He won the Skeena seat by a large majority in 1957 and in subsequent elections.

The Liberal party, understandably, wanted Skeena, but a man could never have beaten Frank Howard in that far-northern riding. What did beat him was television and a woman. Iona Campagnolo was an announcer on a little television station at Prince Rupert, so she had name-recognition and face-recognition with the public. She looked good, sounded good, was bright, and had just that air of competence that impressed the male voter without frightening him. The women voters endorsed her. Iona Campagnolo won that election in 1974 and later became a Cabinet minister.

She defeated Frank Howard for a number of reasons, but the fact that she was a woman gave her an important edge.

PERSONALITY   I do not mean to suggest, by the examples I have given so far, that each candidate should typify the average voter of your constituency. Your candidate does not necessarily have to come from a common mould. You can run for public office a person who is a contrast to the community stereotype. A predominantly Anglo-Saxon constituency, for example, will support a candidate of Chinese, Czech, Hungarian, or Hawaiian ancestry, provided that enough voters can identify with him. Indeed, if you run someone who is "different", you have no trouble getting the face-recognition and name-recognition which you need for voting day.

Samuel Hayakawa, the Japanese-Canadian author, was elected to the U.S. Senate from California. You may remember that he generally wore a Scottish tam-o'-shanter. He took a hard stand against some rioting university students, and the California voters apparently agreed with his views.

Distinguishing features far less outstanding than Mr. Hayakawa's may be enough to give a candidate that quality of recognition, to make him stand out from the crowd, even in a blurred newspaper photograph or on a five-second television shot. One could cite, for example, Abe Lincoln's gaunt face and frame, Robert Stanfield's lantern jaw, Charles de Gaulle's exceptional height. The distinguishing feature may be something that the candidate habitually uses or does: Winston Churchill's cigar, René Lévesque's cigarette, "Flying Phil" Gaglardi's automobile-driving. Even so ordinary an article as a pair of spectacles can be significant. United States Senator Barry Goldwater, who is near-sighted, knew very well the recognition value of the heavy, horn-rimmed glasses he ordinarily wore. So that his voters would not see him bare-faced, he wore an identical pair, with no lenses in them, when reading his speeches.

Such a conspicuous, instantly recognizable feature may, in some constituencies, be worth as much as a thousand votes to a candidate. But certain features may also be liabilities. At the time of writing I would say that a heavy beard would lose 500 votes for a male candidate. Whereas in 1860 you could not get elected without a beard, in 1948 President Harry Truman said, privately, that Thomas Dewey's moustache narrowly defeated Dewey, because the moustache reminded voters of Hitler. Today moustaches are quite acceptable.

A good recognition feature, then, is an asset; yet a glance around any legislative assembly will show that many candidates get elected without it. But some characteristics are essential. A candidate must have a friendly, outgoing personality; he has to like people. He must mix readily and pleasantly with the whole range of people in the constituency: to the intellectuals he must not seem stupid; to industrial workers he must not seem patronizing. He must enjoy public exposure of all kinds, such as canvassing, meetings, interviews, radio and TV broadcasts; and during all such public exposure he must seem credible and honest.

Your candidate will need a thick skin to endure the criticism and the attacks of opponents or the press, as well as of his own supporters.

You may have to search long and hard to find people of this calibre. Good candidates do not grow on trees.

HEALTH   A candidate needs good health. Campaigning is gruelling—lack of sleep, lack of relaxation, incessant travelling, long hours on your feet, and the upsetting of your regular eating habits are inevitable. There is a continuous mental strain, too—the sense of always being on show, of always trying to look dynamic and pleasant while repeating the same things and trying to make them sound fresh and interesting each time. It's like putting on a non-stop performance. The point is often overlooked that if the candidate is not in top physical and mental condition, he cannot do a proper job.

Those who select candidates must bear this in mind. If your candidate breaks down, physically or mentally, halfway through the campaign, there goes all your effort.

POLITICAL   Most candidates in federal and provincial elections
EXPERIENCE   have had previous experience, either as party workers or as local politicians. But experience is not enough and nominations should not go simply as a reward for years of patient plodding to party war-horses who do not possess the other qualifications described in this chapter. Nor should nominations go to complete

political greenhorns—say, a popular athlete or media personality. Such a candidate would very likely find himself in difficulties with questioners at meetings, opponents in political debate, and newsmen. Some political experience, then, is necessary; nominations should go to people who believe in the party policy, who can carry it out effectively, and who can give leadership to campaign workers and to voters.

If you are starting from scratch with a new candidate, trying to capture a seat held by another party, it is a good idea to agree that the candidate will contest at least 2 elections. In the first campaign, your candidate and party will build name-identification and credibility with the voters; in the second campaign, party and candidate will have a better chance of ousting the incumbent.

ENTHUSIASM   I have heard it said that candidates are not supposed to be ambitious, the implication being that ambition is somehow in bad taste. That is all wrong.

The stress of political life is such that, as a rule, only a highly motivated man or woman can get a nomination. Once nominated, a candidate who is not sure that he really wants the job cannot face all the flak of the campaign: the task is so difficult that an indifferent or undecided candidate will surely flinch from it. Then, once elected, it takes a highly motivated person to stand up to all the brickbats of public office. Your candidate needs motivation plus stamina.

REPUTATION   Sometimes an otherwise good candidate is not chosen because of some supposedly discreditable incident in his past: perhaps there is something irregular in his private life, or perhaps he has been in trouble with the law. The candidate's committee must look into such matters. You cannot afford to be taken by surprise if an opponent digs them up and suddenly throws them at you just before polling day.

Yet I feel that nowadays one should not give too much weight to mere private peccadillos. I think most voters are willing to judge a candidate by what he has accomplished, and by what he is now. With many voters, a candidate's family problems may generate sympathy rather than hostility: plenty of people have faced similar problems themselves.

If there is some minor criminal conviction in a candidate's distant past, he should request a pardon. In Canada there is a statutory waiting period after the original conviction and penalty: two years for a summary conviction or five years after the indictable conviction. Then the applicant should contact the local office of the National Parole Board, and apply to the Solicitor General for a pardon under the *Criminal Records Act*. He must wait while the Royal Canadian Mounted Police makes an investigation, which takes several months. Then, if the pardon is granted, the candidate's record is clear.

THE BEST FOR YOU   What sort of candidate will be the best for you—the best to stand as combined teacher and champion to the particular body of voters you have to reach? Remember, you are not looking for a god, just a good candidate who is also available.

It will be useful for the candidate's committee to come up with the names of several people who fit the requirements. Then, to help you decide among them, you can draw up a scoresheet, showing how each one of them fulfils each of the major qualifications listed in the chart below.

First, here are a few notes on the chart. These qualities are not arranged in order of importance. What might be called the "voter appeal" of various qualities or abilities will vary considerably from one constituency to another; moreover, the importance of certain qualities may vary markedly in the same district with the passing of time. I have already commented, for example, on the changing importance of a candidate's sex. I cannot possibly estimate the relative importance of all these qualities in all places at all times. That must be done on the spot. So, opposite each item, give each candidate a score—say,

on a scale from 0 to 10—showing his voter appeal on
that quality, *in your constituency, at this particular
election.*

Quality	Candidate: A Score	B Score	C Score
Integrity			
Gender			
Occupation			
Family (married, single, children)			
Enthusiasm and motivation			
Reputation			
Ethnic background			
Personality			
Platform speaking ability			
Doorstep-canvassing ability			
TV and radio presentation			
Political experience			
Education			
Military service			
Community connections			
Availability			
Common sense			
Totals	_____	_____	_____

NOMINATING
MEETINGS
A candidate may be wisely chosen and well known to
your own members; he must now become well known
to the general public. A nominating meeting can be an
effective first step in that process, if it is used to
maximum effect—that is, if it is timed so as to make a
news story of interest to a large number of voters.

The general rule is "nominate early". By "early" I
do not mean soon after the election has been called; at
that time the media are sure to be preoccupied with
other political news, and your meeting may not
attract much attention. It is better to make the
nomination ahead of the election call, preferably at a
time when there is not much other political news.
That gives it a better chance of attracting attention.
Early nomination also gives your candidate plenty of

time to become known to the news media and to the voters. If you do not already hold the seat, and are putting up a brand-new candidate, this rule of early nomination is especially important.

I would recommend holding a nominating meeting at least 18 months ahead of the election—more if possible. Remember that there is always the risk of a snap election; you should always be prepared for that, with your candidate nominated and already making himself known to the voters.

If you have a sitting member who is to be renominated, there may be advantages in delay. If that incumbent is renominated too early, the voting public will still see him mentioned in the press as "member"; they will still think of him as "member", and will forget that he is also "candidate". So in such a case it could be best to wait till the election call. It then becomes something of a news item that "Joe Doakes", who has already sat in the House for x years, has again been nominated, and now will be fighting his nth campaign.

Occasionally there may be other reasons to delay formal nomination until after the election has been called. As I mentioned earlier, certain public officials have to take leave from their posts immediately on being nominated for any elective position. Usually you would not expect such a person to accept nomination far ahead of the election call, and so lose his income for a period of many months. In such a case it may be possible to spread the word that So-and-so is going to be your candidate, without formally nominating him. This tactic I call having a "twilight candidate".

Considerable thought is required, then, before setting the date of the nominating meeting. It should be done only after careful discussion.

If you are a potential candidate or are supporting a nominee, you must be familiar with your organization's nominating rules. The nominating voters, your supporters, may have to meet certain requirements pertaining to age or citizenship. Above all, they must be organization or party members in good standing: their membership dues must have been paid in accordance with the accepted practice. Even the person who is to nominate your candidate may have to fulfil specific requirements. Check these procedural rules well in advance.

BACKING THE CANDIDATE
Many organizations nominate their candidates, and then seem to forget about them. A candidate, once he is past the excitement of the nomination meeting, needs all the physical and emotional support that he can get. That support serves to alleviate the loneliness that a candidate must feel at times; it also heightens his self-confidence. A candidate who loses his confidence part-way through the campaign is quite a burden. Indeed, maintaining the candidate's confidence and high energy output is vital to success on polling day.

So, once having nominated your candidate, stay with him all the way: he is the best asset the campaign committee has.

A PERSONAL ASSISTANT
A candidate needs a personal assistant. It might be his official agent under the appropriate electoral statute, or it might be some person nominated by the candidate or assigned to him by the campaign committee. Wherever the assistant comes from, his duties will be about the same.

The assistant will see that the candidate does not drift to and from meetings, interviews, or other public activities at random; he will see that the candidate gets to appointments on time, and gets away from them on time. At large functions the assistant runs interference for the candidate and keeps him circulating.

There is the problem of scheduling time for the people who, during the course of the campaign, will be wanting to talk to the candidate, shake his hand, and ask him questions. There are occasions when that is welcome. There are other times when the candidate cannot take it; then the assistant must shield him.

In general, the personal assistant does, and takes the blame for, all the unpleasant things that must be done in a campaign. For example, he writes and signs all the "No" letters. The assistant also does a lot of the good things and lets the candidate take the credit. "Yes" letters, for example, are drafted by the assistant and signed by the candidate.

The candidate's personal assistant is often young, athletic, well-educated, and charming. Whoever he is, he should be a bit of a diplomat, and should have a good sense of time and order.

TRANSPORTA-
TION
I think the campaign committee, whenever possible, should assign a car and driver to the candidate. During an energetic campaign, the candidate needs to be thinking of what he is going to say, not fighting traffic and so running the risk of involvement in an accident. An automobile accident under unfortunate circumstances can have unpleasant results, as Quebec Premier René Lévesque and U.S. Senator Edward Kennedy have experienced.

This job as driver is excellent for a volunteer, and you will probably have several people offering their services. You might see whether the candidate's driver also has the ability to serve as campaign photographer. That is a practical combination.

ALCOHOL
Alcohol-drinking, these days, does not seem to be an ideological issue in the choice of candidates. Whether a candidate drinks or not does not seem to matter. The fundamental question is whether the candidate's drinking interferes with his function as a candidate now and as a member of Parliament, or as a potential Cabinet minister in the future.

John Diefenbaker is a teetotaller and ran Canada tolerably well as its Prime Minister. Winston Churchill drank a lot—some people called him a drunk—but as its Prime Minister he led England to victory in the Second World War.

Alcoholics should not be nominated for high public office. But if your candidate tends to drink too much, at least make sure that he does not get drunk at the wrong times. Watching for this can be part of the day's work for the above-mentioned driver and personal assistant. Drinking alcohol also robs a candidate of his stamina.

MONEY MATTERS   The federal candidate may pay from his own pocket personal expenses not exceeding $2,000; but other than that, he should receive no money, and pay out none, for campaign expenses. Other jurisdictions have different rules on this point, but if your candidate makes up his mind that he will have nothing to do with money, except for his purely personal expenses, he will not get into trouble.

Do not compromise your candidate by getting him involved with the campaign money. A candidate should help raise campaign funds, but he should not handle the cash. The official agent should pay all expenses on behalf of the candidate.

Insist that all campaign personnel conduct themselves impeccably over money matters, so that they can account for every dollar they handle. Then your party will not suffer the embarrassment of a scandal over a $50 hotel bill, or risk your candidate's disqualification over some squalid financial mix-up.

RESEARCH   The candidate must be provided with facts, figures, and other material that will enable him to do the best possible job for the organization. You must give him enough material that he can show himself knowledgeable; but take care not to overload him with facts and figures that strain his memory or make him sound too professional. I have emphasized elsewhere that a simple campaign is the best. A campaign with too much policy content will confuse and possibly alienate the voter.

Unless you have a lot of money, the necessary research will have to be done by volunteers. Here are a few hints on how to organize it.

1. Visit your local library and make yourself familiar with its resources. Get acquainted with the

librarian. Do not be afraid to tell him frankly about your problems: he can help you find the answers.

2. Start a scrapbook, as far ahead of the election as possible. Clip and save every article you can find in newspapers or magazines about your own policy or your opponent's policies.

3. Assemble a committee of knowledgeable people. It can be quite small—maybe only 2 or 3 members—but if possible it should include an elder statesman to advise you. He might be your next-door neighbour, or a former candidate, but he will be able to contribute ideas, and you can bounce ideas off him.

AFTER THE CAMPAIGN
After the election is over and your candidate has won, do not just walk away and leave him to travel alone to the legislature and assume his elected office. A ceremony in which he is presented with a small gift is always appreciated.

And if your candidate has lost the election, it is equally important that you do not let him go home alone, nursing his disappointment. Make sure you thank him for his efforts before you turn him out to pasture. After all, there will be other elections, and you may need him again.

Win or lose, if there is a surplus in the campaign funds, you might give the candidate an allowance for out-of-pocket expenses or lost salary. But watch the statutory requirements and be sure to read your electoral statute for details of what is permissible.

A LONG-TERM PROJECT
This business of choosing and assisting your candidate will very likely fail for you if you delay starting until the election is announced and if you quit the effort as soon as the result is declared. Once you have that candidate's committee formed, it can very well stay in existence between elections, studying how people in other jurisdictions have selected and are selecting candidates.

It can be a fascinating study. Who would have thought that Franklin Delano Roosevelt, crippled by

polio, who smoked cigarettes in a long holder and
who liked wearing a cloak, would score such a
victory in the U.S. presidential election of 1932; or
that John Fitzgerald Kennedy, a millionaire New
Englander, would win the hearts of poverty-stricken
black Americans? And in Canada, who would have
thought that Pierre Elliott Trudeau, a French-speaking
Catholic intellectual and bachelor, would win the
votes of so many conservative Anglo-Saxon voters?

I recently came across what I consider is a good
description of the qualities that a political candidate
should have. It was written by the philosopher and
mathematician Alfred North Whitehead: "Men
require of their neighbours something sufficiently akin
to be understood, something sufficiently different to
provoke attention, and something great enough to
demand admiration."* I suspect that these are the
qualities that men seek in their leaders.

*Quoted in Basil
Wright, *The Long
View* (London:
Secker and
Warburg).

Your Campaign Plan

YOUR CAMPAIGN COMMITTEE HAS BEEN APPOINTED;
YOUR POLICY HAS BEEN NAILED DOWN: AND
YOUR CANDIDATE HAS BEEN NOMINATED.
YOU NOW NEED A CAMPAIGN PLAN.

I am a strong believer in the effectiveness of written, detailed, step-by-step plans. A reasonably intelligent, literate person can safely be left to do almost anything, from servicing a truck to cooking an omelette, if he is given precise, orderly instructions. The same principle applies to political campaigning: to get the best value from volunteers' time and talents, give them detailed plans of what they are to do. Even the experienced campaigner need not scorn the written plan. *He* may know exactly what to do, but perhaps his assistants do not. Or perhaps he may fall sick part-way through the campaign and have to hand over his duties in a hurry to someone else. It is handy, then, to have a written record of what has been done and what is still to do.

Written plans enable the election planner to conceptualize the whole campaign from beginning to end. The planner and the candidate *know* how the campaign is going to end. Written plans and written instructions also allow you to train huge numbers of volunteer helpers quickly. In addition, written procedures prevent an angry or uppity committee chairman from walking out of the organization with his regional campaign plan in his head. The campaign manager keeps a copy of the original plan of attack, and so can quickly instruct new personnel.

Written instructions, no matter how simple, enable

you to create on paper the whole campaign months or years ahead of the event. Written instructions and written conceptions enable you to nail down all the small details and leave the candidate and the campaign manager free to be more flexible and creative should events demand it.

Several kinds of plans are required for a successful election campaign.

THE LINEAR   I use the term "linear" because this plan can very well
PLAN   be drawn up in a long straight line, on which dates indicate the passage of time and brief notes remind everyone of things to be done. You can see an example of a linear plan on page 215. But in some circumstances planning can be done vertically. Anyway, the important thing is to create the plan; horizontal or vertical, it reminds everybody of the deadlines to be met and the things to be done by those deadlines. Vertical plans can be used for mechanical events like closing the voters' list, and horizontal plans can be used for psychological pacing, like timing display advertising in the daily newspapers.

If you are beginning well in advance, you might have a linear plan that starts 18 months before an election. A similar plan might begin on the day the election is called and end some time after polling day, when the result is declared final.

In provincial elections many of the basic steps are prescribed by law. Here are some examples.

A BRITISH   *PROVINCIAL ELECTION ACT,* REVISED STATUTES OF BRITISH
COLUMBIA   COLUMBIA, CHAPTER 306, 1960, 1966, AND 1975.
PROVINCIAL
ELECTION

Days Till Poll	*Required Action*	*Section of Act*
38	Writ issued by Chief Electoral Officer and Lieutenant-Governor	40
30	Closing Day, voters' list closed	12(4)

Days Till Poll	Required Action	Section of Act
27	Court of Revision of voters' list	17(3)
15	Nomination Day	33:54
5,4,3	Advance Poll	114(4)
0	Polling Day	44
-13	Final Count	121
-21	Last day to apply for recount 8 days after Final Count	130(4)
-33	Last day to present a Petition to the Court to void an election 21 days after Final Count	203(b)

A FEDERAL ELECTION

CANADA ELECTIONS ACT. CHAPTER 14, SUP. 1, 1970.

Days Till Poll		Required Action	Section of Act
58	(Sat.)	Chief Electoral Officer issues Writ Advertising prohibited	61.2
56	(Mon.)	Returning Officer distributes Proclamation	19
54	(Wed.)	Candidates nominate enumerators	18A(4)
49	(Mon.)	Enumerators prepare preliminary voters' list	18(1)
45		Judge (Section 2) appoints revising officers	18A(27)
44	(Sat.)	Enumerators complete preliminary voters' list	18A(21)
42	(Mon.)	Enumerators post and deliver preliminary lists to RO	18A(25)
30		RO announces date of advance poll	92(3)
29		Candidates nominate revising agents	18A(68)
28		Four-week advertising period begins	61.2
26	(Wed.)	RO completes printing preliminary lists	18(5)
25		RO sends candidates preliminary voters' list	18(12)
23	(Sat.)	RO mails printed preliminary lists to individual urban voters	18(15)
21	(Mon.)	Nomination Day (except in far north) and appointment of Official Agent	22(5)

Days Till Poll	Required Action	Section of Act
19 (Wed.)		
18 (Thur.)	Revision of voters' list	18A(39)
17 (Fri.)		
9 (Sat.)	Advance Poll	92(2)
7 (Mon.)	Advance Poll	92(2)
2 (Sat.)	Advertising prohibited for two days	61.2
0 (Mon.)	Polling Day	
-3 (Thur.)	Official addition or Final Count	53(2):19(3)
-7 (Mon.)	Last day to request recount	56
-9	To present Petition to a Court to void an election, please see *Dominion Controverted Elections Act*, R.S. of C., 1970	

RO = Returning Officer

In addition to these legal requirements, there are other things you will want to do for a good campaign: canvassing, holding public meetings, recruiting and training scrutineers, printing publicity material, and making arrangements to get out the vote, etc. I need not list them all here. They are described elsewhere in this book, and the requirements of one constituency may differ from those of another.

But some plan there must be. The campaign committee must define the critical events, set a date for each one, draw up the plan, and then *act* on it. To omit some of the legally prescribed items may immediately knock your candidate out of the running and so waste all your preliminary work; to omit or delay some of the other tactical items may seriously injure the campaign.

A well-drawn plan will make optimum use of the time available—time that always seems too short. It *is* possible to turn a community around; you *can* change public attitudes; but it requires efficient use of the time, money, and human energy that you have at your disposal. Such efficiency can be attained only by planning.

THE STRATEGIC
PLAN
The linear plan described above sets out the day-by-day activities of the campaign. But there is also another plan, extending over a longer time and describing in broader terms the strategy by which your campaign is to be conducted. This strategy must be worked out far ahead, before you can draw up any linear plan.

Here, for example, are some typical issues to be considered for this strategic plan. Will you attack hard and carry the battle right into the enemy's camp, or will you just ignore him? How are you going to open your campaign? Should you pick one program plank and hammer hard on that because your constituency is vitally interested in it? How should you pace the campaign? When are you going to hold your most important meeting? What issue should you choose to close your campaign?

I shall be dealing more fully with such matters later in this chapter. Here I want to emphasize that they must be considered early and thoroughly by the wisest, most experienced people in your organization if you are to formulate a good strategic plan.

THE SINGLE-
PLANK
STRATEGY
A strategy that has often been successful in appropriate locations is to begin the campaign by picking one plank in which your constituency is vitally interested. You then keep on hammering that plank right through to the end of the campaign.

Here is an example. Randolph Harding lived near Slocan Lake, approximately 80 km north of the B.C./U.S. border and 170 km west of the Alberta/B.C. border. He was first elected to the B.C. Provincial Legislature at Victoria for the Kaslo-Slocan riding in 1946. His specialty and expertise was the Columbia River Treaty between Canada and the United States. He was opposed to many details of the agreement which was finally reached. He believed that different dams should be in different places, and that Canada's share of the downstream benefits should be returned to Canada in the form of electric power rather than in money. As an opposition member, he fought the government all the way.

When the treaty was signed and the Columbia River dams began to go into place in Mr. Harding's riding, he switched his emphasis to protecting those people who would be flooded out as the water rose behind those new dams. Although Mr. Harding dealt equally well with other issues, that one-plank strategy kept him in Victoria for twenty-five years! Some admiring colleagues used to call the Harding campaign "How green was my valley!"

For an example from the United States, consider the presidential primaries of 1968, when Senator Eugene McCarthy won millions of votes by emphasizing the one issue of opposition to the Vietnam war.

COMPLEX STRATEGIES However, the single-plank strategy may not always be the best strategy. Different places, different political situations, may call for more complex plans. Take, for example, my own campaign for mayor of Vancouver in 1970. There were three main candidates: Mr. Tom Campbell, Dr. Bill Gibson, and myself.

It was a bitter campaign in a turbulent period. The FLQ crisis in Quebec had led to proclamation of the War Measures Act in Canada and, as a result, the army was patrolling the streets of Montreal. James Cross, the British Trade Commissioner, had been kidnapped. Pierre Laporte, the provincial Minister of Labour in Quebec, had been murdered. In the United States students had been shot and killed at Kent State University.

In Vancouver, Tom Campbell, the incumbent mayor, was waging a private war with the young people of the city. The flower children of the 1960s were still with us, and Mayor Campbell was taunting them. He had issued three-foot nightsticks to the police and was threatening to enforce the War Measures Act in Vancouver, too. It was the fall of the year, the city was restless, and all candidates were having a difficult time. Because of the tense political situation my party and I decided to proceed very carefully.

In Vancouver voting day is scheduled for a certain day every second year, so we had been able to set out the linear plan, the time sequence, quite easily. Formal policy was no problem, either; that had long ago been defined within the party structure. What we were concerned with was campaign strategy. We required a strategy that would be effective for the limited time and resources we had at our disposal, and that would be appropriate to the difficult political situation that I have just outlined. Our campaign strategy was:

1. Establish that we would be capable administrators by quietly explaining our civic program.

2. Establish trust with the electorate before going on the attack.

3. Accuse Mayor Campbell of dividing the city by probing old wounds.

4. Explain that all people had a common interest in conserving the city.

5. Ask the voters not to vote for Mayor Campbell.

6. Appeal to common civic pride in Vancouver and ask the voters to vote for our candidates.

Thus we planned to appeal to the common hopes and fears which unite people and to create a positive image for our candidates and a negative one for our opponents. Mayor Campbell was creating a siege mentality, and we planned to capitalize on it.

A complex strategy like this requires that the candidate's speech-making be carefully planned. Should he have one all-purpose speech, dealing with all planks at every meeting? Or should he expound one plank at a time at different stages of the campaign, and in different locations? These decisions should be made early in the campaign.

Now let me offer a couple of examples from the United States. When Nelson Rockefeller decided to run for his fourth term as governor of New York State, a public-opinion survey was taken eighteen months before election day to find out what ordinary people thought about him. The survey showed that the majority of the voters would not have voted for Nelson Rockefeller if an election had been held then. Although much had already been accomplished in the state of New York under Nelson Rockefeller, the ordinary voter did not associate these successes with the name of their governor. So the Rockefeller campaign committee set out to identify Rockefeller with the exciting things that had been done in the state in the preceding twelve years. That took a long time, but as election day approached, more public-opinion surveys were taken, and it was found that the electorate had indeed changed its mind. It had identified the achievements with the man, and on election day Nelson Rockefeller was returned as governor.

The story of the John Lindsay campaign for mayor of New York is also interesting. That campaign was based on many local-neighbourhood, auton-omous, storefront committee rooms. Every storefront had a full-time local campaign manager, and each storefront had its own plan, geared to its own community. One storefront campaign committee actually distributed leaflets along one bus route early each morning to the passengers awaiting the perennially late bus. The leaflet said something like "When John Lindsay is Mayor, the No. 7 bus will run on time."

A similar strategy might well be applied in a widespread Canadian constituency, where each locality has its own special problems. In each place emphasize what is most important to the voters there; do not distract them by harping on matters of interest to voters a hundred miles away in different geographic and economic conditions.

PACING THE CAMPAIGN You have chosen your candidate and defined your policy; you know how much money and how many volunteers you can expect for your campaign. Now the problem is when and where to utilize these limited resources so as to create the maximum effect on the voters at the right time. A good election campaign is, in many ways, like a good play, film, or TV show. It starts slowly, gathers momentum and credibility, and saves its denouement for the eve of polling day.

Do not peak too early. In that 1970 Vancouver civic election Dr. William Gibson, understandably provoked, started his campaign by calling Mayor Campbell a Fascist. As Brian Campbell, our campaign manager, said, "What does Dr. Gibson do for an encore?"

Peaking too early means that you can only expect your campaign to go downhill from then on. A premature peak can result from defective strategy, as in the example just mentioned, or it can occur if you run out of money or ideas or volunteer workers partway through the campaign. It can also occur if you overwork the candidate in the early stages; then he gets tired, feels dejected, and drags down the entire campaign effort. Plan to conserve the candidate's strength. So long as he feels energetic and cheerful he can help spur his party on.

Many factors must be considered when you are deciding just how to pace your campaign. For example, when are you going to hold your first public meeting, and what issue or issues should be raised there? When, if required, will you inject new issues into the campaign? When are you going to make your most important policy statement? Just when, and where, should the candidate be doing what? When should you bring your campaign to a peak for maximum effect on the press, radio, and TV, and hence on the voters?

And, of course, the campaign must not suddenly stop at its peak. So how are you going to bring it to a close?

In my view the right time for bringing your campaign to its peak is about 60 to 36 hours before the polls open. It's important to remember, though, that other candidates will certainly be trying to do the same thing at the same time, and it may be difficult to get the media attention you need.

In the aforementioned mayoralty campaign, polling was to start at 8 a.m. on Wednesday, December 9. On the previous Saturday, December 5, I created an important news story by stating that civic disorder would break out in Vancouver if Tom Campbell was re-elected as mayor. On Monday, December 7, we held a dinner, hoping that the daily newspapers would report the speeches on Tuesday so that the voters would read them before going to the polls on Wednesday. The media ignored it and, as a result, our actual peak was reached at 11:40 p.m. on Monday, December 7, with an hour-long television debate among the three mayoralty candidates.

Next, I would like to give an example of campaign-pacing over a much longer period. In Chapter 3, when the question of trying to win a seat held by another party arose, I suggested planning for a new candidate to run for two or more successive elections.

The provincial Mackenzie riding is not really rural, yet it is certainly not a city constituency. My friend Donald Lockstead had run once against the incumbent, Mrs. Isobel Dawson, and came close to winning. After that defeat, the Mackenzie party organization sensibly elected Donald Lockstead as their president, so that, until the next election, he would have a good platform from which he could discuss local issues. Then, late in 1971, he was again nominated as candidate for the Mackenzie riding. The election was to take place in June 1972, giving Lockstead six months to campaign.

By the time of that second nomination, Lockstead knew a lot about the business of campaigning; and because of the good results in the last election, he was within striking distance of victory. So he began a quiet, relentless campaign. It appeared that if he looked straight ahead, enunciated party policy, and met enough people, he would walk into public office.

1. POLICY.   The candidate drew up a list of problems which needed attention in the constituency. Then he

made public announcements on these issues, writing
letters to various ministers of the Crown, both federal
and provincial, and forwarding copies of these letters
to the local weekly newspapers, thus creating news
stories. He started slowly, and increased the tempo of
his announcements as the election drew closer.

2. MEETING PEOPLE.   Mr. Lockstead aimed to pick up
votes one at a time by tirelessly meeting voters and
shaking hands. This was his strong point. For the
purpose of maximizing his efforts, he concentrated on
those polls in which research and experience indicated
that he had good support. For example, he attempted
to call personally on every household in the
Municipality of Powell River, and I think that he
succeeded.

This was a well-paced campaign plan, without risk,
without much expense. Donald Lockstead thoroughly
understood his own riding and adapted the party
policy to local needs. He literally elected himself to
the legislature one vote at a time. It remained for the
party machinery to get out the vote on polling day,
which they did.

This strategy of building the campaign to a
precisely timed peak must, as I said, be carefully
worked out far in advance. Finally, though, it calls for
more than a paper plan, more than a capable
candidate. You must keep your campaign workers
informed and keep them enthusiastic. The candidate
should, whenever possible, be in the committee room
in the evening when the canvassers are returning from
their calls on the voters. Canvassing is a tough
business and the candidate needs to give all the
support he can, by canvassing himself some of the
time, and by meeting the canvassers at the end of
their day. This encourages the staff, and the candidate
also hears first-hand what the canvassers have been
learning on the doorstep. A bottle of beer, a bottle of
pop, a doughnut or two, and the relating of the
hilarious events of the past twelve hours is part of the

immense fun of politics. It enriches all who are involved in it.

I have said a lot about choosing strong planks to build the structure of one's own platform, and I have discussed the timing by which those planks should be presented to the electorate. But what about your opponent? What are you going to say about him and his platform? And when?

It might seem that the obvious thing to do is to attack, and keep attacking; but the obvious thing is not always the best. For example, if you are campaigning against an unknown candidate, you should never attack him, because to do that would publicize him, his party, and his campaign. Of course, the converse applies: a little-known candidate can publicize himself by attacking a well-known candidate.

If you are planning to attack an opponent, you should decide carefully just when to deliver the attack. If you attack prematurely he may be able to reply and smooth the subject over, with the result that, by election day, the voters have forgotten all about it. Your major attack, then, should be timed so as to produce its maximum effect close to election day.

As for the subject of the attack, it is best to keep clear of your opponent's strong planks and attack at his weakest point.

Remember, too, if you are a serious candidate, and there is a possibility that you will be successful in the election, *you* will be attacked at your weakest point. If you have planned to expect and counter such attacks, you need not be upset when they come. So analyse your own platform and your personal qualifications dispassionately; pick out the weaknesses and prepare ahead of time how to repel attacks on those weak spots. Whenever possible, plan how to turn such attacks to your own advantage.

It is always necessary, then, to keep an eye on the

opposition and to hold a little of your own time and strength in reserve. When your campaign is working well, and when your organization is not overreaching itself, you have the flexibility to take advantage of an opponent's unexpected mistake or to repel an unexpected attack.

FINANCIAL
PLANNING

Not least important among the various aspects of campaign planning is the need to use your money as effectively as possible. This financial planning, too, should be done well in advance, and should be based upon geographic, social, and political factors in your own constituency, upon a dispassionate analysis of results obtained from various expenditures in previous campaigns, and upon a realistic estimate of how much money you will have to spend next time. Here are some sample plans.

THE $500
CAMPAIGN

Let us begin with three campaigns which cost $500 or less.

1. Have a business card printed with the candidate's name, address, and phone number on one side, and a short statement of your program on the other side. The candidate should go to all the joint meetings of candidates, when invited. Make suitable press releases available to the media on printed letterhead stationery; use the same stationery to write letters to opinion-leaders in the community; and hold small social gatherings in your own home. Save your best news-release till 4 days before polling day.

2. Put 2 advertisements in a weekly or community paper. Place one ad early, appealing for help and funds, and place the second advertisement as close to the election as you can, depending on the publishing deadline of the neighbourhood newspaper.

3. Spend $500 on one poster and spend all your time nailing up the posters as they are torn down by your opponents and small children. Order at least 2,000 posters, since once the basic production costs are paid for, extra paper and press time cost little. Design your poster as essentially a display advertisement of 8

words or less, but have a small statement on policy in 8-point type underneath your picture. This is the size of type usually found in the body of newspaper stories.

THE $2,000 CAMPAIGN

1. Be courageous and select 1 positive plank for your program. You might even create a campaign slogan for yourself, such as "One-Tax Tommy", or "More Parks for People", or "People Not Freeways", or "Save Chinatown". Your next task is to design 1 brochure which explains in some depth your approach to the problem. If you are running on a 1-plank platform, you should go into the policy in considerable detail. The front page of your leaflet should be simple, containing 8 words or less, but the interior of the leaflet can be as full of material as a magazine, though not too crowded.

2. You could conduct an entire campaign by publishing a newspaper all about your candidate's policy and family. Have a good look around your community and see whether a small newspaper will agree to publish a special edition for you, or a special central section on your campaign. You might go to your local union, fraternal organization, or professional group, and because your campaign is integrated with their public policy, they may agree to feature your campaign. You could create your own newspaper for one issue, if you could not adopt an existing publication. Ask your party to put out a special edition of their publication for you, and perhaps for some other candidates. One benefit of integrating your campaign with an existing, recognized periodical is that you might receive inexpensive mailing privileges.

THE $10,000 CAMPAIGN

A $10,000 campaign gives you more scope, though all campaigns benefit from simplicity and integration. Here are 3 possible shapes for the campaign.

1. Rent and staff a committee room in the busiest part of town. Find an empty shop which is between tenants and centre your campaign on the storefront.

Decorate the windows dramatically with white newsprint and bright poster paints, but make sure that the public can see the whole interior of the shop without difficulty, and take positive steps to get members of the public off the street and into the store. A sign might say "Come in and see whether you are on the voters' list", or perhaps "Free coffee and doughnuts", or "Meet the candidate personally every morning 9-11 a.m.".

Section 66 of the *Canada Elections Act* makes it an offence to offer food or drink with the intention of inducing any person to vote in an election, so go easy on the free coffee and doughnuts, or have a prominently displayed box for donations. During one campaign in Vancouver Centre, we placed a very large fishbowl full of crumpled two- and five-dollar bills in the front window of one of our storefront committee-rooms. The campaign manager used to prime the fishbowl every morning with paper money and not very many coins.

Round out your campaign with a series of newspaper ads spaced and worded for final effect.

2. Design a bumper-sticker on paper, which can be glued to the inside bottom area of the rear window of an automobile. You can have your printer apply glue over the bumper-sticker or request your supporters to use translucent tape. You can also have a bumper-sticker designed to affix to the outside bumper of the automobile, using rubber cement, but the simple paper strip is more conveniently mailed, inexpensive, and more easily removed after election day. The effective use of this paper bumper-sticker depends upon access to a large mailing list, or the purchase of a large mailing list from a commercial establishment. The voters' list is not always available early enough. It is possible to mail such a bumper-sticker to every automobile owner in a given area. The inside of a bumper-sticker can have a full statement of your program printed on it and instructions on how to affix it to the window. The exterior view of the strip should have only 2 or 3 words on it. Hold your

bumper-stickers back for the last 3 weeks of the campaign and try to have them all go up on the windows on the same day. At least you can use this sort of timing and emphasis with your own supporters. Check motor-vehicle regulations which may prohibit blocking of windows.

Blow the rest of your $10,000 on 1 newspaper ad published 48 hours before the election, and feature a duplicate of your bumper-sticker in the advertisement itself, preferably in the same colour as the bumper-sticker.

3. Use most of your money to get a warmly worded and personally addressed letter and envelope into every voter's home, and buy a large ad in a newspaper 48 hours before the election, reproducing the letter in the ad. The advertisement might read "You have received my letter in your home, please vote for me at the polls."

Getting Started

IT ALL DEPENDS ON HOW MUCH TIME YOU'VE GOT.

Let us suppose that the probable date of the next election is 18 months away. The candidate's committee has made its choice; the campaign committee has been appointed. You want to get going right away. Here are some items to be considered by those two important individuals, the campaign manager and the candidate.

CAMPAIGN MANAGER'S PROGRAM OF ACTION

1. The event that kicks off a campaign is usually the party nominating meeting. That meeting is too valuable to be wasted, so organize it properly. See that there is a good turnout. Try to create an atmosphere of quality and dignity; show that your candidate is confident and capable, that he knows what he is doing, that he really is the sort of person worthy of occupying an important public office. Have the media people invited well ahead of time; if they do not show up, at least see that they receive detailed, accurate reports of what happened.

2. Although the campaign manager, and perhaps one or two other administrators, may be paid, the campaign is going to be run mainly on volunteer help. Start enlisting people willing to work. Lists of volunteers who helped during the last election should have been kept; check them. Spare no effort to find more volunteers. Names and addresses of supporters

who will work for you or donate money to your campaign are invaluable.

3. Have your campaign committee meet fairly frequently from the start, so that members get to know each other. When you are getting organized early, meetings should be held in private homes; food should be served, and a light atmosphere created, so that the team can develop an *esprit de corps*, something you are going to need when the going gets tough at the height of the campaign.

4. Sit down with the candidate and draw up a program of "quiet presence" for him. If he is already an alderman or a member of the legislature, he has an excellent platform from which to talk to his constituents. If your candidate is out of office, he will have to work a little harder to keep his name before the public.

The campaign manager will be alert to see that the candidate is invited to speak at meetings around town that need a speaker or are sympathetic to your candidate: for example, visits to other constituencies and to universities, political meetings, and fraternal gatherings. If there are not enough such prearranged meetings available, a good campaign manager will organize the occasional lunch or house party where the candidate will speak briefly. Right from the start the candidate should try to keep his name constantly before the voters. It is equally important that, in the early stages of the campaign, the candidate not come on too strong; he must pace himself, like a long-distance runner.

Detailed suggestions for the candidate in this very important matter are offered in Chapter 6, "The Candidate and the Public"; but the campaign manager should keep an eye on the candidate's activities, should make every effort to help him, and, if he is a novice, should tactfully instruct him.

5. For anyone writing or talking about winning elections it is unfortunate that there are two radically different procedures with the same name,

"nomination". I have already described how a candidate is nominated by his party, and have recommended that, as a rule, it should be done well in advance. But that party nomination alone will not assure that the candidate will run in the election: he must be "officially nominated" to have his name on the ballot.

There are precise legal requirements for this official nomination. Do not leave it to the last minute. Call on the Returning Officer of your electoral district. Find out from him the exact procedure for this official nomination and personally see that it is carried out. If you forget it, or bungle it, all the rest of your campaign efforts are wasted.

One Conservative candidate at Prince Rupert found, just before the deadline, that his nominating petition did not bear enough signatures of registered voters. He suffered the embarrassment of having to hustle up more signatures in the local beer parlours. I have also known at least three candidates who just never got officially nominated.

As soon as the candidate is officially nominated, you must also appoint, and report to the Returning Officer, an official agent and an auditor for the campaign. Here, too, certain local requirements must be met. Check on these with the Returning Officer well ahead of time.

6. Establish a basic collection of records and reference material. Here are some items that will be useful.

(a) A constituency map showing the polling divisions. This is usually called a poll map.

(b) A telephone book, or books, which covers the whole constituency. Also any available street directories. If you live in a rural area, the post office will sell you a list of people receiving mail at that post office or on the rural routes at a reasonable cost. Get a booklet from the post office on how you must prepare unaddressed householder mail.

(c) A voters' list. If the current voters' list is not available, obtain a voters' list from the last election.

(d) Poll-by-poll results of the last election in your constituency. These are available from the Chief Electoral Officer; they will be useful for planning your canvassing.

(e) Any text you can get your hands on about electioneering in general or about your constituency in particular.

(f) A list of your own members and close supporters.

(g) A list of your own officers and campaign committees, with full names, addresses, and phone numbers.

(h) A number of copies of a biography of your candidate (about 250 words in length) and pictures of your candidate.

7. Start to get your supporters on the voters' list. In many jurisdictions there is a permanent voters' list and a person may register at any time. If you enumerate a neighbour or get him on the voters' list, your chances of getting his vote later on are high. It is also a sound public service to persuade people to get on the voters' list. In federal elections there is a special enumeration just before each election, because Canadians move around a lot. Voter-enumeration is an important legal formality. There is nothing mysterious about it, but it must be done properly. So make an appointment with the Registrar of Voters and have a chat with him. Tell him you want to help, and ask his advice.

8. Notes for speakers are an important part of the campaign ammunition. Some speakers' notes are usually prepared at a provincial or national level by experienced campaigners; but, as I have already said, party platforms may sometimes have to be modified to suit local conditions. Also, in municipal and other kinds of elections there may be no top-level source of speakers' notes.

Your own editor of speakers' notes should be appointed a year ahead of the expected election call.

He takes the policy, as established by your policy committee, and creates notes for 1-minute, 5-minute, 30-minute, and longer speeches. He also provides verbatim material for radio and TV spot advertising or commercials. The longer speeches in particular need to be well spiced with pertinent facts, anecdotes, etc., to keep them interesting.

Although the editor starts far in advance, he cannot sit back and consider his work finished until the campaign is over. At any time some public event, some statement by a party leader, or some challenge from the opposition, may call for quick revision of speakers' notes.

The editor will need adequate reference material. Here are some suggestions.

(a) A copy of your organization's political policy. If you cannot get a new one, get hold of an old one.

(b) Abundant facts about your own locality. The *Canada Year Book* is one good source; more details and recent figures can sometimes be obtained from Statistics Canada. Most areas have published local histories. The local library may also have useful material.

(c) A financial report of the government unit for which your candidate is running. For example, if it is a provincial election, you will need the public accounts for the last fiscal year and also a copy of the Minister of Finance's last budget speech. This material will supply statistics for speeches.

(d) Many other government reports will be useful to your constituency or your candidate. Gather any that bear on areas or issues of interest.

(e) Facts about the opposition will be useful. Try to get policy statements and annual reports of opposition parties. Collect embarrassing quotations from opponents' speeches. If your opponent is Minister of Transport, get his annual report, and read Hansard for the period when his estimates were before the legislature.

(f) Have a simple filing system for miscellaneous material: news clippings, jokes, wise sayings from statesmen or philosophers, short verses, etc. It is better to have too much spare material than too little.

Good speakers' notes, prepared early, guide the experienced candidate and improve the performance of an inexperienced candidate. Moreover, such notes will guide campaign-committee members who are designing leaflets, posters, and street signs and writing press releases. A sound political campaign is one in which all media are co-ordinated, for, if candidate contradicts canvasser or leaflet contradicts poster, then you and your party are in trouble.

Much depends on the editor of the speakers' notes; so the campaign manager must try to support him in every way.

CAMPAIGN MANAGER'S CHECKLIST

1. When will the candidate be nominated by his party? When will the nomination petition be signed and filed with the Returning Officer?
2. Has the campaign committee been appointed, and who is its chairman?
3. Has the campaign budget been approved?
4. Has a special election bank-account been opened and who are the signing officers?
5. Where is the campaign headquarters going to be located?
6. Who is responsible for designing and printing the candidate's poster?
7. Who is responsible for designing and printing the basic campaign leaflet?
8. Has necessary time and space been reserved on billboards, radio, and television?
9. Has material been purchased to permit the design, printing, and erection of lawn signs or street signs?
10. Canvassing:
    (a) Are we entitled to propose enumerators to the federal Returning Officer?
    (b) Do we have poll-by-poll results from the last election?

(c) Do we have a constituency map and do we have a poll map?

(d) How many complete canvasses will we attempt in this constituency?

(e) Who is compiling a list of the canvassers?

11. Candidate's itinerary:
    (a) Is the candidate to have his own personal canvassing card or leaflet?
    (b) Is the candidate going to give aggressive leadership in door-to-door canvassing?
    (c) Are we going to organize coffee parties with the candidate?

12. Who is responsible for headquarters design and location? Are we going to establish satellite committee-rooms?

13. Do we have a copy of the *Elections Act* and instructions?

14. Finance:
    (a) Budget control
    (b) Responsibilities of the official agent
    (c) Receipt books, official and temporary

15. Getting out the vote:
    (a) Who is going to design the canvassing kit?
    (b) What should be its contents?
    (c) Are the usual poll-book markings acceptable?
        S = supporter
        P = possible supporter
        H = hostile
        U = undecided
        O = out or not at home
    (d) Establish school for canvassers.
    (e) Can we afford a full-time poll-organizer?

THE RETURNING OFFICER   You will be having a lot to do with the Returning Officer, before and after the election, so it is good to know in some detail who he is and what he does.

Once the Prime Minister decides to call an election he advises the Governor General to dissolve Parliament. If the government is defeated in the federal House, the Prime Minister *must* advise the Governor General to dissolve Parliament. When

Parliament is dissolved, the Chief Electoral Officer causes to be issued a writ of election which appears as Form Number One in the back of the *Canada Elections Act*. This writ of election is signed by the Chief Electoral Officer and is mailed to the Returning Officer in each electoral district. The constituency returning officers are permanent officials who are appointed after a new government takes office, so that they are constantly standing by in the event of dissolution of Parliament.

The Returning Officer has specific duties under the *Canada Elections Act*. Publications called *Instructions for Returning Officers* and a *Manual of Information* are issued by the Chief Electoral Officer and are obtainable from his office at 440 Coventry Road, Ottawa, Ontario, K1A 0M6. They contain a diary of duties of returning officers and a diary for candidates and their official agents. These two last-named diaries will assist you in planning your critical path plans for the campaign. Campaign managers and candidates need not get bogged down in the details, but should use them to get the overall picture. You only need to study them in detail if a specific problem arises. The official agent should be a close student of the diaries and the *Act*. A copy of the official diary for candidates is in the Appendix.

THE CANDIDATE'S PROGRAM OF ACTION

As the candidate you will not want to carry around with you the detailed diary. Here is a simple plan showing the essential things you must do between the start of the campaign and election day. Write out the plan and check off the items as you accomplish them.
1. Your party has to nominate you.
2. You need a campaign committee.
3. You need to alert, or to build, a party structure.
4. You must get your supporters on the voters' list.
5. You must get officially nominated; are you qualified?
6. You need a basic leaflet or poster.
7. You have to be visible.

8. Run for office in your own party or become the president of your ratepayers' association, so that you can speak with authority on issues as they unfold.
9. Do not forget to register and vote.
10. Persuade your supporters to vote for you.

The Candidate and the Public

YOU DO NOT HAVE TO BE NICE TO EVERYBODY,
BUT IT HELPS.

I don't believe there need be a dichotomy between
being a good candidate and being a good elected
member. I credit Lester Pearson with being the first
modern Canadian who did not change his persona
when he became Prime Minister. Mr. Pearson allowed
himself to be himself, so he gave future political
candidates in Canada the opportunity to be
themselves both on and off the platform.

No matter what the candidate does or does not do
in his public life, he must first be himself. He must
allow his own personality to shine through his policy,
his literature, his photographs, and his speeches.

John Squires, MLA for Port Alberni, B.C., was a
good candidate and a good member. He had been an
alderman for Port Alberni; he earned his living in
the woodworking industry on the west coast of
Vancouver Island. His constituents were loggers and
fishermen. He had a craggy appearance and an honest
verbal delivery which was convincing. Premier
W. A. C. Bennett always listened carefully to what
John Squires had to say, even though they were from
different political parties, because Mr. Bennett,
shrewd man that he was, believed John Squires to be
an authentic voice from Vancouver Island. Good
politicians are hungry for facts and ideas and are alert
to receive them, wherever they come from. As some

unkind people have said, politicians sit on the fence with one ear to the ground.

I suggest that, for a candidate, the appropriate contortion is to keep one eye on his constituents, and the other on himself. He must always be conscious, not only of what he is doing and saying, but of how he does and says it: he must estimate the possible effects of all those words and actions. He is playing on a big stage, before a big audience. So in this chapter I shall describe how a candidate may project himself, his policy, and his party, right to the back row of that large auditorium, his constituency.

THE NOTEBOOK   Every candidate should buy a cheap notebook that fits in an inside pocket or a purse. Use it as a diary of events; forgetting appointments creates a very bad impression. In the book you can note matters in the constituency which need remedies, and record the names, addresses, and telephone numbers of those people who would like to assist you. Such contacts are invaluable. The notebook should stay with you during the whole campaign, and when the final results are in, it will be filed away with your other mementoes.

SYMBOLIC ACTS   A candidate must be conscious of the value of symbolism: it has enormous influence in political life. Let us look at some examples.

Do you remember when President Lyndon Johnson turned out the lights at the White House? That was before the energy crisis. He wanted to impress upon America that he believed in economy, and in spending the taxpayers' money carefully.

Can you remember Vice-President Hubert Humphrey playing with his retarded granddaughter in that thirty-minute television film broadcast to the United States just prior to the 1968 presidential election? He climbed thirteen percentage points in the public-opinion polls in thirty-five days to lose narrowly to Richard Nixon.

Can you remember the telephone call that President
John F. Kennedy made to Mrs. Martin Luther King
when her husband had been imprisoned in the South
for civil-rights activities? Kennedy could not interfere
with the criminal law of a southern state, but the
nation knew, and the blacks in the South knew, that
the President was concerned.

Do you remember reading about Mahatma Gandhi's
walk to the sea in 1930, to publicize his opposition to
the salt tax being imposed on India? That symbolic
act by Gandhi did not cost much money and did not
require a professional public-relations adviser, but it
galvanized India, and startled Britain, too, before the
days of television. Gandhi's walking, and his
spinning, were symbols.

Here are some symbolic acts I performed as a
candidate and as legislature member for the British
Columbia provincial riding of Mackenzie. In my first
election I hired a fish-boat to visit the smaller polls. I
donated books on Canadian subjects to local high
schools. I asked the schools to nominate one or two
of their pupils to receive expense-paid trips to Victoria
to see the legislature. One such young lady arrived at
Victoria very upset because her luggage was missing; a
telephone call from me to the president of the airline
recovered the suitcase. I enrolled in law school and
received a law degree. This resulted in some attention
from journalists.

To protest an increase in telephone rates, I
inaugurated a pigeon-post service from Powell River
to Vancouver. When I was travelling by myself on an
airplane, I purchased accident insurance to finance a
by-election, should my estate collect the proceeds of
the insurance policy.

I voted, alone, against the *Equalization Assessment
Act* when the other forty-seven members of the
legislature voted for it. I had been advised by the
Municipality of Powell River that the legislation was
not suitable for them. To speed construction of a road
along the north side of Howe Sound, I walked its

length, seven miles, with the superintendent of construction.

Symbolic acts often involve making interesting trips, opening new buildings, walking in parades, and being photographed with distinguished non-politicians.

The things a candidate says, on the platform and person-to-person, are important, of course; yet I believe that the public is more impressed by *acts* than by *words*. A publicized telephone call, a photographed walk, a human gesture such as the picking up of a child, can create a mood, or evoke trust, both more powerful than the most impressive speech.

Note that word "publicized". Many actions are good in themselves and, of course, are worth doing for that reason alone. But for political purposes, for the winning and maintaining of voter support, actions must be publicized. So do not be bashful. See that those symbolic acts are reported by the news media; see that they are photographed and that those photographs go to local newspapers, and to industrial or professional magazines.

But you must also be constantly aware of alienating voters. If you are not sure whether some action, slogan, or joke is in good taste, avoid it.

DRESS AND PHYSICAL APPEARANCE   I cannot lay down detailed rules concerning the candidate's dress, but the subject is an important one, and deserves some discussion. Most voters will see you only once during a campaign, and from that one glimpse they will form their impression of you. Dress contributes significantly to that impression.

Dress may be symbolic. Remember the western movie where the villain wore a black Stetson and the hero a white one? President Jimmy Carter wore that old sweater on television to remind voters that he is just one of the guys. Pierre Elliott Trudeau is not afraid to wear a rose in his lapel.

One theory is that the candidate should imitate the dress of the community—that if most of your constituents are riverboat gamblers you, too, should dress like a riverboat gambler. I do not agree with that. I do not really think that loggers expect you to turn up for a public meeting dressed like a logger. Mind you, I do not think they would like gold cuff-links or perfumed hair-spray, either.

Generally I wore a plain, dark business suit. Dark clothing gives psychological weight to a candidate. Moreover, dark clothes photograph well in black-and-white and televise well in colour. When appearing on television be careful not to wear clothing with very small patterns; it causes annoying visual distortions called "moiré effects".

During the 1960 American presidential race a debate between Richard Nixon and John Kennedy was broadcast. People who heard it on radio thought that the two debaters came out about equal. But television showed a youthful, fresh-looking Kennedy, matched with an ill, tired Nixon. That contrast gave Kennedy the tiny edge which meant victory for the Democratic party. Nixon had a painful knee injury, and had paced himself wrongly.

INFLUENTIAL
PEOPLE

It is the candidate's job to move around and meet people of influence in the constituency. Go in and have a long talk with the postmaster. There are special regulations which must be followed if you are going to do mass mailing.

See your local clergyman; tell him that you are a candidate in the election and that you wish to ask his advice about certain matters.

Go and see the editor of your local paper and ask him how he wants the news to come in. Do not hesitate to ask his advice. Treat him as a professional and he will extend the same courtesy. It is important never to assume that someone is opposed to you. Be polite and friendly to everybody, friend and foe alike.

You might even drop in and meet the local opposition. Ran Harding told me that he always called on his opponents when visiting the small towns in his riding. He always had something pleasant to say to them. As a result, although many disagreed with him, few disliked him.

LETTERS AND
TELEPHONE
CALLS

Efficient handling of mail is an important feature of the campaign. A candidate should have a simple, dignified letterhead and business card. He should write personal letters to people in the community on issues which concern them.

When a candidate sees things that need to be done in his local community, he should write a letter to City Council, or to the minister of the Crown in charge of the problem, being careful to get his facts straight and to be reasonable in his request. After the recipient has had sufficient time to study the letter, a copy should be given to the local papers, so that they can turn it into a news story if they wish. Never release a copy of a letter to the press if the letter is of a private or confidential nature.

A candidate must have stenographic services, and it is up to your campaign committee to supply these services. Often a volunteer will be pleased to look after the candidate's mail.

You must reply to every letter that comes in, if possible on the same day you receive it; often short, handwritten notes are sufficient.

Write letters to the editors of newspapers within the constituency: not too many, and not too complex. In each letter, deal with one subject that particularly concerns readers of that newspaper.

Make sure that the telephones in your own home and at headquarters are answered promptly, and that all names, numbers, and messages are accurately recorded. Since you will probably be out much of the time, campaign staffers can take messages all day. In the early evening retire to a quiet corner and respond to the day's calls unhurriedly. Candidates, like judges, must be patient.

PERSONAL
CONTACT

The most exhausting aspect of every campaign is the personal contact between the candidate and his constituents. It is a wearying but rewarding business, both personally and politically.

If intensive canvassing techniques are to be used in your constituency, the candidate should also canvass. This gives leadership to your workers, and keeps the candidate in contact with the thinking of the voters. Some candidates have tried to personally canvass every household in their constituencies.

A candidate can turn up at his local union meeting or ratepayers' meeting, say a few words, and try to get it reported in the media. When there is a public event, or quasi-public event, such as a wedding or a bridge-opening, the candidate will be present like other members of the public, so that he can see and be seen. Leo Nimsick, the British Columbia opposition MLA for Cranbrook, always went to provincial government "openings" whether he was invited or not. He would bounce up on stage and sit down; then one invited guest would be bewildered to find no chair for him. I do not recommend this unless you are my friend Leo Nimsick.

Moreover, while you are trying hard to reach the uncommitted voters, do not forget to maintain contact with your own supporters. Entertain small groups in your home. Do not be afraid to have fun. An election is too important to be taken seriously all the time.

Use the telephone. Phone around the constituency once a week to your top people; ask them how the campaign is going and tell them your views about the progress of events. Ask for their advice and listen carefully to it.

LIBEL AND SLANDER   Once officially nominated as candidate in an election, you will of course be enunciating the general policy of your party and specific policies concerning your own constituency. You may also want to attack the policies of your opponent, to criticize his past record in Parliament or legislature, and to comment on his fitness or unfitness to hold office. This is a perfectly proper campaign procedure, but some care is needed.

If you want to avoid trouble, it is useful to have some idea of the law regarding libel and slander.

A libel is a printed or written statement, or a picture, maliciously published to defame a person, i.e. to damage his reputation in the minds of right-thinking people. A slander is a similar malicious, defamatory statement that is only spoken, but not put in writing or print. A person who believes you have libelled or slandered him may have you summoned before a court of law, and there claim damages for the alleged injury to his reputation. You can defend yourself against civil libel or slander by affirmatively proving that your statements are true.

Unfortunately, the law of libel and slander is not all that simple. A person who is a member of a legislature enjoys what is called "absolute privilege" *while speaking within the legislature.* No matter how false or malicious the statement he makes there, he cannot be sued. However, a member who makes such statements may be disciplined by his fellow members. In any event, such an unscrupulous person eventually has to face the voters who elected him.

Newspapers also have statutory protection from libel suits when they are accurately reporting on public meetings.

The attitude of the courts differs markedly between libel and slander. Let us describe them separately.

1. In a libel case the court assumes:
    (a) that the written statement is untrue;
    (b) that it has indeed damaged the reputation of your opponent.

For a defence, then, the onus is on you to prove that the defamatory words are true. This may be a difficult task, and if you fail to do it, you have lost the case.

2. In a slander case the court also assumes that the spoken statement complained of is untrue, and was spoken with malice. But there is no automatic assumption that the words have damaged the reputation of your opponent. It is up to him, if he can, to prove his damage. That usually means that the

opponent's friends and colleagues will go into the witness box and say they have thought less of him, or ceased to do business with him, after hearing your untrue verbal statement.

Here again, your defence must be to prove that the words you spoke were true.

Nevertheless, even if you cannot prove that what you said was true, you may, as a candidate in a public election, have what the law calls "qualified privilege". If, during an election campaign, you make a statement which is relevant to that election, or is the sort of thing which voters are entitled to know in order to enable them to cast an informed ballot, you are protected against the law of defamation if you believed the statement to be true, had carefully checked your material, and had no malicious intent towards your opponent. The law takes this view to encourage vigorous debate during elections and to provide the public with as much information as possible about the issues being discussed.

Suppose, for example, that in a public meeting you read a clipping from a reputable newspaper containing damaging statements about your opponent which you later found out were not true. You could plead in court as a defence that you believed the information in the clipping to be true, that you read the clipping to a meeting of voters to assist them in making their choice, and that you bore no personal malice towards your opponent. In other words, you wanted to help the electors and not merely to harm your opponent.

Once a defendant has proved his qualified privilege, then the plaintiff must prove actual malice to be successful in a defamation suit against a candidate. I would emphasize that it is up to the defendant to prove this qualified privilege; and the rules are fairly strict. If you have not yet been officially nominated, or if the election has not yet been called, you might have difficulty.

The other legal umbrella of the public figure is "fair comment". A person in public life may express his opinions on matters of public interest, such as an election issue, a stage play, or a work of art. The four essentials of this defence of fair comment are:

1. The words must be comment or opinion, and not mere assertions of fact;

2. The speaker or writer must be careful to state accurately the original facts upon which he wishes to comment;

3. The words spoken or written must be a matter of public interest;

4. The words must be spoken or written, not from malice but from a desire to inform.

For example, if a candidate in a political election criticized an opponent for the purpose of damaging his business rather than to inform the electors on issues in the election, then the candidate could not claim he was making fair comment. So remember that a motive of ill will or spite will destroy the umbrellas of qualified privilege and fair comment.

If at any time a candidate finds himself accused of defamation, he should not hesitate to seek legal advice. And a candidate should, of course, conduct himself and his campaign in a way that minimizes the risk of getting into any such difficulties. Here are some specific suggestions.

1. A good rule, in commenting on an opponent, is to discuss only his public performance: his speeches, public actions, decisions in court, and matters of public record. Say nothing about his private life—even if he is a drunk or an alleged drunk. Do not speculate on his motives for saying or doing anything; just concentrate on the words and actions themselves.

2. Unless you are confident you can prove it, be careful not to imply that an opponent is unfit for, or negligent in, his occupation; to defame a person in his occupation is a serious libel. For example, do not describe a lawyer as crooked, a clergyman as immoral, or a public official as dishonest unless you have indisputable proof.

3. You must also avoid defaming products or corporations. It can be dangerous, for example, to say

or write, without proof, that Brand X detergent injures the skin of people who use it, or that ABC Enterprises Limited is swindling its stockholders.

4. The courts have ruled that you cannot defame a group or class of people. Therefore it is usually all right to say harsh things about another political party, a government, or perhaps the cabinet. Yet, even in attacks upon groups, care is needed. For example, in a big city it may be safe to say that the police are taking bribes; but if there is only one policeman in the town, that statement may well defame that individual policeman. If you are morally certain of your facts, but your evidence is thin, it is better to talk about "those guys" or "the opposition" or indeed "the government".

5. If you are a candidate without much experience I advise that you concentrate on positive policy and only criticize individual opponents on their public record. Look up parliamentary reports and use your public library. Quoting from reputable newspapers is usually safe; but remember, a reporter or a newspaper is sometimes wrong. If the newspaper has defamed someone, you also will defame him if you quote it.

6. Be fair. Even in criticizing your opponent for his public actions and attitudes, you should never offend the public's sense of fairness. Contrary to what some people believe, the public is very fair. They really do not like you criticizing a politician's private peccadillos; electors have their own frailties and can sympathize with a candidate who has his fair share of human weakness. It is a good thing to win an election, but you may also have to face the electors another time. So, out of respect for them, and for the sake of your own conscience, try to keep your reputation for fairness intact.

7. If you do make a mistake, as we all do sometimes, and you find something you have said is untrue, do not be afraid to admit the mistake and to apologize publicly to the person you have wronged. There is no use in clinging stubbornly to the error; if you do, the opposition will hammer at your fingers

until eventually you must let go. A quick retraction of the false statement and a graceful apology will kill the political issue and let you get on with the rest of your campaign. Such an apology may even increase your political stature.

BANNED BY THE CBC
My one and only brush with the law of defamation was when I criticized a British Columbia minister of the Crown for not doing his duty. I accused him of not acting in the face of wrongdoing by a fellow minister. The offending minister had sued a Vancouver lawyer for defamation. This is not an unusual tactic, by the way: a person in public life issues a writ against a critic for the purpose of shutting him up. In all likelihood the matter never goes to trial, but the criticized public official can plead innocence and frighten his opponent into silence.

At that time the Canadian Broadcasting Corporation had a valuable policy of allocating free time to political parties with members in the legislature. I was then a member, and the caucus had assigned me to do one of those free-time broadcasts.

I arrived at the CBC studios on Vancouver's Georgia Street and presented my script for a run-through. The producer then told me that the Corporation had, on legal advice, decided that there could be no comment on their radio network about the charges and counter-charges concerning this minister, because the relevant civil suit was in progress and any comment on the matter would, they feared, be equivalent to contempt of court. As a result, they could not allow me to proceed.

To be quite frank, I was delighted to be banned by the CBC; it was almost as good as being banned in Boston. I marched out of the CBC studios and down to the *Province* daily newspaper, where I presented my script to Bruce Larsen, who was then their night city-editor.

He heard my story, read the script, and looked at the clock on the wall. It showed 7 p.m. The evening deadline for their first morning edition was 9 p.m. He

phoned the publisher and, after a quiet conversation that I could not hear, he smiled and said,
"Well, so far it's one to one." I understood him to
mean that he and the publisher were split on whether
the material should be published.

The city editor next phoned the newspaper's lawyer,
then said to me, "He's going to the office to look at
his books and he'll phone us back."

I waited. An hour later, the lawyer phoned back.
The editor told me, "You've accused the minister of
nonfeasance of office." After that had been explained
as a failure to perform a duty I said, mildly surprised,
"I've been accusing him of that for years."

Anyway, the lawyer advised against publication, so
the *Province* did not print my analysis of the
accusations; but they did say that I had been banned
by the CBC.

CRIMINAL
DEFAMATORY
LIBEL

There is another, more serious, form of libel that is
described in Section 262 of the Criminal Code. A
criminal defamatory libel is the publication, without
lawful justification or excuse, of material that is
likely to injure the reputation of a person by exposing
him to hatred, ridicule, or contempt, or that is
specifically designed to insult a person. A criminal
defamatory libel could be described as an assault
against a person in written words. Note particularly
that it is no defence against this kind of charge to
prove that what you said is true. A criminal
defamatory libel may be true or untrue; the point is
that it is an act which endangers the public peace, and
is therefore a crime.

Here are two examples of things that have been
held to be criminal defamatory libels: a letter
containing an immoral financial proposal to a virtuous
woman, because the letter might reasonably tend to
provoke a breach of the peace; or a newspaper
description of jurymen at a trial as murderers.

One rarely sees anyone charged with this crime
these days since public debate is much calmer than it
was years ago. A person in public life who uses

common sense and good taste in discussing political issues is not likely to infringe this part of the criminal law. Do not write or do things which are so outrageous and so inflammatory that they may cause public disorder.

THE UNEXPECTED   Despite your best efforts at planning, the occasional event for which you are not prepared will still happen. One thing that always adds a little spice to a campaign is the sudden exposure of something discreditable in a candidate's background. This sort of thing tends to give candidates premature grey hair and heart-attacks.

The opposition usually holds the accusation back until the last three or four days of the election campaign, so that the candidate or the party will have difficulty in replying before polling day. This manoeuvre is called a "roorback". The dictionary defines roorback as an untrue statement, but in politics it has come to mean an unfair, last-minute accusation which is not relevant to the issues at stake in the campaign. Cleverly done, a roorback is very difficult to reply to.

In one campaign, I was due to appear on a morning phone-in radio program, a format that I rather liked. Ten minutes before I left for the radio station a supporter phoned me at home.

"Ed Broadcaster is going to confront you with Joe Co-candidate's criminal record," he said.

"Okay," I said. "Thanks for phoning."

I arrived at the station and the program started. Over Ed Broadcaster's shoulder was a huge studio clock, and I watched its hands turn for a full hour, waiting for the exposure. The question came at last. "Did you know that Joe Co-candidate had such-and-such a criminal record?"

"Yes," I answered. "I'm aware of the man's criminal record. He has completely reformed, and we're glad to be part of his rehabilitation," or something to that effect.

Political candidates have to be ready for these emergencies. In this case a ten-minute warning made the difference between a barely adequate response and what might have been a disaster. In politics or war a little knowledge goes a long way, so make sure that you keep a candidate informed. And make sure that, if trouble is brewing, he is not the last person to know.

GO SLOW   I have urged an early start in campaigning. That does not mean starting off in a furious rush. Go slow. It is better to begin at a pace that you can sustain throughout the campaign. Do not make a statement on five different subjects at the same time. Remember, you are building recognition and credibility and trying to create a deep, sharply defined impression in the mind of the public. Try to organize a routine so that quietly, and more or less regularly, you are brought to the public's attention; so that more and more of them come to identify you as a candidate, to know who you are, what party you represent, and what policies you stand for. These should be your main objectives.

Public Meetings

MEETINGS SHOULD BE CAREFULLY PLANNED.

Some people in politics do not like public meetings; they feel that it is more effective, and cheaper, to concentrate the campaign effort on literature, advertising, broadcasting, and canvassing. There is, admittedly, a certain risk; an unsuccessful meeting can injure the campaign, and even unsuccessful meetings are time-consuming and cost money to organize. Then perhaps a candidate does not like meetings because he realizes he is not a good speaker, feels ill at ease before an audience, and thinks he would be using his time better in door-to-door canvassing. Indeed, I have known of some political campaigns conducted without a single public meeting.

Even so, the potential benefits of meetings outweigh the risks. A candidate for public office has to appear in public sooner or later, and he may as well do it at a meeting that he can organize and control. A good meeting can be a sort of showplace to kick off a campaign, or to bring it to a powerful climax. A successful meeting:

1. Gets you media coverage.
2. Interests new voters.
3. Stimulates and encourages the candidate.
4. Lifts the morale of your election workers.
5. Makes you visible in the community.
6. Gives you the chance to go on the record about campaign issues.

These things result from a successful meeting, and the success or failure of a meeting is largely in your own control; it takes only a little more thought and work and money to run it properly than to bungle it. Here are some hints towards making every meeting a success.

CHOOSE THE HALL WITH CARE

There are 2 factors that often lead the organizers to choose the wrong hall.

1. An excessive desire to economize. I certainly do not advocate wasting money in any aspect of a campaign, but skimping on hall rentals is a false economy if it results in an undesirable location or building.

2. An unrealistically high estimate of attendance. As a result, you get a hall that is far too big, the audience looks lost among the empty seats, and such a meeting seems to be a failure.

It is best to hold meetings in local hotels, rather than in drafty community halls or echoing school gymnasiums. In the hotel you can have luncheon or dinner meetings, as well as straight platform-and-speaker-type meetings. One hundred people in a pleasant dining room designed for seating one hundred and ten is a success. Two hundred people in a cold hall with seats for four hundred looks like a failure. It is certainly a failure of election planning.

And, properly organized, the cost is moderate. If you hold a luncheon or dinner meeting, you can sell tickets ahead of time, guarantee a full house, and make a small profit. This will ensure the success of your meeting. If you cannot sell a hundred tickets for lunch, do not run for public office.

Here is an example of a meeting spoiled by being held in a bad location. When Lester Pearson was leading the Liberal party, his party was foolish enough to hire and attempt to fill the large, ugly old Forum in Vancouver. It was a building more suitable for horse shows and hockey games than for political meetings. The place was filled all right, but many were opponents of the Pearson administration. The organizers did employ an orchestra, which created a good mood at the beginning of the meeting. Unfortunately for them, the Forum was furnished with solid wooden benches rather than chairs, and the opponents banged their heels against those benches all evening, creating a sound like the roll of distant thunder. It was disconcerting, and ruined the buoyant effect that the election planners were trying to achieve.

DECORATIONS   Whatever kind of hall you choose, it should definitely be decorated. There is no need for great expenditure of time or money. Even a bowl of flowers will give life to the occasion; though do not place the flowers so that they hide your candidate. If your opponent is there, place the flowers in front of him.

One big poster or banner displayed at the front of the hall is useful. "Vote for Smith", or "Jones for Burrard", or just the name of your party: any of these looks effective and, once procured, can be used repeatedly. You can roll it up and put it in a suitcase. A large picture of your national leader on the left of the platform and an equally large picture of your candidate on the right is good business; it implies that they are both in the same league. An organizer putting together a speaking tour for a national leader should give some thought to simple hall decorations.

This decoration heightens the drama of the occasion, but it is not provided just to give the audience something to look at. It also prepares for the possibility that pictures may be taken for the newspapers or for television; you want to create an appropriate frame or backdrop for the candidate's face—something that will help to convey your message to everyone who sees the photo. If you do not have a suitable backdrop, the photographer will create one. It is better to create your own backdrop. Note that hotels always have their name placed on the front of the speaker's podium or reading desk. Hotels are conscious of the fact that this name will appear in the media. Watch for it in newspapers or on television.

You should place your own sign on the podium as well—a sign you will be proud to see on the nightly television news.

APPOINT
MARSHALS

It is the responsibility of every organization holding a meeting to make sure of maintaining order. If you cannot police your meeting, do not hold one. You should have at least 2 marshals or ushers for each 100 people you expect. Here are the functions they will carry out—functions that will ensure the success of the meeting.

1. They should get to the hall at least 2 hours early to see that doors are open, lights are on, ventilation or heat is working, chairs are conveniently set out, and the public-address system is in operation. These things should all be done before the first members of the public arrive. It creates an impression of inefficiency if such details have to be patched together by the marshals while spectators are waiting.

If your marshals do not attend to these matters, it is possible that the opposition will. Opponents have been known to get to a meeting hall first and turn up the thermostat to 30°C on a hot summer day, or turn the furnace off when it is below freezing outside.

2. Marshals should be identified by small, discreet insignia—badges or armbands.

3. If pre-sold tickets have to be checked or collected at the door, try to do it quickly, so as to avoid long line-ups. If last-minute ticket sales are likely to be made, someone should be there with tickets and change, ready to make such sales at a moment's notice. The good effect of a meeting is heightened if everything goes like clockwork right from the start; confusion about admission procedure can create an impression of inefficiency for the party and the candidate.

The marshals should show the spectators to the seats as they arrive. At public meetings, they should always make sure that the first 2 or 3 rows are filled with supporters. They should also see that noisy opponents do not pack the forward rows of seats for the purpose of disrupting the meeting. Disrupting meetings is an offence under the *Canada Elections Act*, Section 71.

The marshals should show reporters to the seats or tables reserved for them, and watch to see that nobody else butts in on that space.

If, by mischance, it looks as if the audience is going to be too small for the hall, the marshals should move the people who are there towards the front as much as possible, and try to remove empty chairs. This reduces the bad effect of the small turnout. If extra chairs are needed, marshals can help the staff of the hotel or meeting hall to set them out as quickly as possible.

4. If leaflets or other printed items are to be handed out, the marshals do this.

5. If, during the meeting, there are any signs of trouble, the marshals should move close to the disturbance; their presence will likely prevent any serious disorder. If it becomes necessary to eject serious troublemakers, the marshals do this, under the general direction of the chairman. At a large meeting the chairman can delegate authority to a head marshal. The purpose of the marshals, however, is to *prevent* trouble. A smile, a joke, a polite hand on the shoulder can often deflect trouble and win friends.

6. The marshals take up a financial collection if that is required.

7. One marshal, fully familiar with the public-address system, should stand by the control mechanism throughout the meeting to adjust it and keep unauthorized persons away. This marshal should test the system and know where to get quick help in the event of a breakdown.

8. After the meeting, the marshals do whatever is necessary to leave the hall in good order. This is important; the owner of the hall and his maintenance staff will judge your organization by the condition in which you leave their hall. Creating good impressions is the essence of your campaign.

MUSIC Live or recorded music before and after a meeting can have a good effect on the mood of your supporters, and on the public. A bored or depressed audience is a severe handicap for any speaker; a cheerful, interested audience is a bonus for the speakers and a step forward for your campaign. The function of the campaign is to create a favourable emotional reaction towards your candidate, your platform, and your party. Well-chosen music can be a great help. Live entertainment is such a rarity these days that it creates a nice impression.

The meeting will, of course, be opened with the National Anthem; there is no point in letting the other candidate appear more patriotic than you are. Consult your musicians beforehand about the sort of music that will be suitable for your particular audience.

CHOOSE A
COMPETENT
CHAIRMAN
Being chairman of a public meeting is a full-time job; you cannot be a good chairman and simultaneously be preparing refreshments, or selling tickets, or signing up new members, or distributing literature. The chairman may be sitting still and silent for much of the time, but he must be attentive to what is going on, and must be ready for quick, decisive action on any problem. The chairman is running the meeting, and nobody else.

The general manner and conduct of the chairman, too, can contribute a lot towards the success of a meeting: a weak chairman can severely impair the work of good speakers. A capable chairman can compensate for a weak speaker.

Get a strong, experienced chairman. The actual campaign is no time for breaking people in to this responsible position. If your organization is short of chairmen or speakers, a training school can be started early, as a long-term campaign strategy. It is fun, too.

AGENDA You should aim for a "shape" to the meeting which is pleasing and effective. This requires a carefully prepared agenda. It is the chairman's job to draw up this agenda well in advance.

INTRO-
DUCTIONS AND
THANKS
The chairman is responsible for seeing that each speaker is introduced and thanked, either by doing it himself—the simplest way—or by getting someone else to do it.

This important task is frequently bungled. While Premier of Saskatchewan, Tommy Douglas was asked to address a meeting in the community hall at Central Butte, Saskatchewan, 110 miles northwest of Regina. There had been blizzard warnings all day, and people were advised not to use the roads, but Douglas set out anyway, by car. After considerable trouble the Premier arrived and a delighted mayor led Mr. Douglas forward for an introduction. "Mr. Premier," said the mayor, "we are delighted you came. We know how busy you are in Regina; we know how terrible the weather has been. We tried to get a poorer speaker, but we couldn't find one!"

Long introductions are a bore to the audience, and are generally disliked by speakers themselves. I once criticized a good friend of mine for making careless introductions, which went something like this: "You all know Bill. Here is Bill Jones." Soon after I mentioned this to him, he was to introduce M. J. Coldwell, MP, at a meeting in the town of Powell River, British Columbia. My friend dutifully wrote to Coldwell's office. They mailed him three foolscap sheets of biographical material and at the meeting he read *all* of it.

The proper way to introduce a speaker is somewhere in between. A good introduction will:
1. Give the speaker's correct name. I have heard chairmen give introductions without mentioning the speaker's name. If the main speaker is a candidate, his name should be mentioned several times. If there is the least doubt about any part of the name, check it carefully with him and *write it down*.

2. Give the speaker's rank and title, e.g. mayor of the city. Even though you and most of the audience may know the speaker well, you cannot assume that everybody does.
3. Give the exact purpose of the candidate's speech. If the chairman does not know the purpose of that speech, the meeting is in trouble. A well-prepared, well-delivered introduction is designed to smooth the way for the main speaker and make his task easier.
4. End with the formal call upon the speaker: "It now gives me great pleasure to call upon Mr. Smith," or some such phrase. This call provides the speaker with a helpful cue so that he can begin his speech elegantly.

In preparing an introduction, it is useful to ask the speaker himself if there is anything he particularly wishes to have mentioned, or if there is anything he would rather have omitted. Make notes for your introduction to avoid the risk of forgetting the details. Even if you are introducing your own brother, still speak from notes.

The expression of thanks after a main speaker has finished is usually brief. A grateful, good-humoured reference to some point that the speaker made is not amiss, but the thanker should certainly not be allowed to ramble on into a speech of his own. This also applies to chairmen.

CONTROL
TIMING
I think that 2 hours is long enough for a political meeting; evening sessions should start at about 8 p.m. and should run no later than 10 p.m. Whatever the schedule, make up your mind that you are going to start the meeting on time. Enthusiastic supporters, talking among themselves, may not mind a ten-minute delay, but to that uncommitted voter, sitting silently by himself, it seems like a long time. Punctuality, moreover, is one of those symbolic actions that I mentioned earlier. Critics may question the promises of efficiency and economy coming from an

organization that wastes time and cannot run a meeting properly.

Starting and finishing on time is especially important at luncheon meetings. At that time of day many of your audience will have other appointments to keep, so if your meeting starts late and drags on too long you will have people walking out just as the candidate reaches the high point of the speech.

At any meeting at which a meal is to be served, ask the hotel management or the caterer for a close estimate of how long it will take. Use this in advance in drawing up your time plan. Get started on the main part of the meeting as soon as possible after the meal is over. It is better that a few of the chairman's opening remarks should overlap with the last stages of coffee-serving or table-clearing than that there should be a delay in which nothing is happening and the audience is beginning to feel bored.

Here is one more application of that principle. Just occasionally there may be an unexpected holdup during a meeting: a delay in meal service or a candidate who has been delayed. For such occasions it is very useful to have in reserve a speaker who can be relied on to jump up and give a lively 5-minute or 10-minute speech, and yet who will not feel wounded if he is not called upon. This is a good role for the "elder statesman" type of supporter. And it is very comforting for a chairman to have such a reserve speaker available.

Some speakers are able to control the timing of their own speeches; others are not. The chairman must see that the meeting does not run on too long, that all the introductions, main speeches, thanks, announcements, collections, refreshments, and so on, are finished on time. It can be difficult if some members of your audience become bored and restless; if some of them start walking out, the effect is disastrous.

Whatever your schedule and time limit are, discuss them in advance with your speakers, and agree on how much time each is to have. When each speaker has agreed to his own time limit, advise him that you will hold him to it.

Some speakers are grateful to have the chairman give them a signal when they have 5 minutes to go. This can be a hand-signal that is visible to the speaker, but not to the audience.

If signals do not work, you will have to interrupt the speaker. You should have agreed on this procedure prior to the meeting. It would be absurd, of course, to interrupt a main speaker who has run over his time, but who is going like a house afire and has captured the attention of the audience. But any speaker, major or minor, who has gone overtime, and who is boring the audience, robbing time from another speaker, or otherwise jeopardizing the success of the meeting, should be controlled. First try passing him a note. The chairman should always have pen and notepad handy. Often there are newspaper or TV deadlines to be met, and the chairman simply must be in charge of the meeting. If all else fails, the chairman can turn off the public-address system.

DISTURBANCES   Keep an eye on sources of trouble. An experienced speaker may very well be able to dominate the meeting himself, without any action on the chairman's part. Many speakers have a stock of all-purpose replies, good for almost any situation.

W. A. C. Bennett, former Premier of British Columbia, always had exciting meetings. He always got a full house, often of opponents. In the 1963 provincial election he became so annoyed that he threw a copy of the budget speech at a heckler. An alert photographer caught the printed booklet in mid-air, and W. A. C. Bennett was once again on the front page.

If the speaker is capably handling a disturbance, there is no need for action by the chairman; but if the speaker seems to be losing control, the chairman should at once rise and request that the interrupters be quiet. The effectiveness of a chairman and his marshal assistants depends largely upon timing. A discreet act early on can be worth a lot of force later.

You may chair many meetings without ever having such a scene, but keeping order is one of the chairman's most important functions, and he should be prepared for it.

QUESTION TIME   If there is a pause when questions are called for after the main speaker has finished, the chairman may need to start the ball rolling by asking a question himself. Always have this question prepared in case it is needed.

If you suspect that a question from the floor has not been heard by all the audience, then repeat it clearly, so that everyone knows what it is the speaker is about to answer.

If a lot of people want to ask questions, select them in random order, from different parts of the hall. This heightens audience interest.

If questioning lags, do not struggle to prolong it by pleading for more questions; close the meeting. It is better to have a meeting finish a little early than to keep it going too late.

END ON A   It is very important that you give some thought in
HIGH NOTE   advance to the way you should end your meeting. The strongest possible ending is an appeal for specific help. People like to help in a campaign, but they have to be asked. A brief, strong appeal for help should be delivered by the chairman or a main speaker, and a book should be available at the back of the hall where volunteers can leave their names, addresses, and telephone numbers.

A meeting which has strengthened your organization is a success. That is a mark of good leadership.

MEETINGS AND   Some organizers and candidates seem to be shy about
MONEY   the subject of money. That is poor strategy. Appeal for funds at every public meeting.

While you can make good use of money in your campaign, there is another reason for making the appeal. The public knows by now that it costs money to finance an election campaign. If you don't ask your audiences to assist you in raising money, they are going to start wondering just where you are getting your money from.

It has been my experience that if you tell people what you are using the money for, they will contribute to your election expenses. Take the audience into your confidence as far as campaign funds are concerned. Treat the voters as mature people. Appeal to them according to your best judgment of their ability to contribute. Do not be overcautious. If you ask them for five dollars a head, that is probably what you will get. If you ask for only twenty-five cents, you will probably get that too. Always have blank cheques on hand.

The financial appeal should be made by one of your best speakers. A good time to appeal for funds is after an inspiring speech by your main speaker, but before questions from the floor. Thank your main speaker, then make a short, effective appeal for funds. While the marshals are passing the hat, the chairman can invite questions from the audience.

MEETINGS AND THE MEDIA

Do your best to make each meeting into a *news event*. Invite the media people personally in good time, by letter. Let each of them have:

1. A biography of the candidate;
2. A photograph of the candidate;
3. A direct quote of about 300 words from the speech that the candidate is going to give. This should concentrate on some subject that is new or particularly timely.

Give reporters an opportunity to interview the candidate apart from the main audience. If he is not going to say something topical, do not invite the press. Yesterday's news is no news!

(More details on dealing with the media are given in Chapter 9.)

MEETINGS AND
THE OVERALL
PLAN

Meetings should not be allowed to become repetitions of the same old show. Each meeting should have something about it that is new and different, even surprising. This will help to maintain your regular supporters' interest, as well as arouse the interest of the media and of the general public. A successful election campaign is often a campaign of calculated risks. The candidate should plan his speeches and interviews accordingly: consult with him on this point. A successful campaigner is innovative.

I believe that a good tactic is to deal with only 1 main policy subject at each meeting. I have heard some criticism of this method, but I suspect that comes mostly from supporters who are already familiar with the whole platform. However, the speaker is not aiming his meeting primarily at his supporters: he is trying to inform, to convince, and to convert people who are not yet supporters—people who read or listen to the news media. If you offer a potpourri of policy items at each meeting, you will not reach these new people effectively. Remember, too, if you are speaking three times a day for thirty days you will have to have an all-purpose speech, but you will also have to spice that speech once a day with a new angle.

For example, in a civic campaign, typical issues, each good for one day, might be: housing, taxation, pollution, rapid transit, social welfare.

The ideal meeting is a blend of the old and the new. Never be afraid to hammer away repeatedly at the basic theme of your party's platform.

So keep up the basic summary of your position, and give 1 new main issue at each meeting. Many of these issues can be planned ahead of time, and the dates of their introduction can be decided in advance. This planning gives pace and drama to your campaign. For other new, controversial material, watch the campaigns of your opponents: they are sure to say, or to print, items that will need challenging or denouncing. If it is a slack day, it is always a help to view something with alarm. Conflict is a powerful means of arousing public interest; well-chosen, well-timed conflict is a sure-fire way to get good value out of public meetings. Do not be afraid to attack, if your facts are carefully correct and your conscience is clear.

(For most of the items it will be desirable to include names and phone numbers of the persons responsible.)

1. Hall chosen and booked ☐
   (a) Address recorded ☐
   (b) Rent paid ☐
2. Chief Marshal appointed ☐
   All marshals recruited ☐
3. Banners or posters ordered ☐
4. Other decorations, if any, ordered ☐
5. Music arranged ☐
6. Chairman appointed ☐
7. Agenda decided ☐
8. Advertising ordered ☐
9. Meals, refreshments, etc., ordered ☐
10. Media invited:
    (a) Advance publicity information supplied ☐
    (b) Space arranged in hall ☐
    (c) Interview facilities arranged ☐
11. Schedule for any visiting speaker confirmed—especially national leader ☐
12. Transport for speaker arranged, if required ☐
13. Financial arrangements made:
    (a) Ticket-selling ☐
    (b) Fund-raising ☐

(The chairman does not necessarily make all these arrangements himself, but it is advisable that he should know what they are.)

1. Meeting place, date, time decided ☐
2. Supporting personnel checked:
   (a) Marshals ☐
   (b) Musicians ☐
   (c) Sound technicians ☐
   (d) Registrar for volunteers ☐
3. Arrangements for arrival and departure of main speaker made ☐

4. Agenda decided ☐
5. All speakers appointed or checked:
   (a) Introductions, thanks, etc. ☐
   (b) Main speaker ☐
   (c) Appeal for volunteers or for membership ☐
   (d) Financial appeal ☐
6. Written time-schedule prepared ☐

Campaign Literature

"A POWERFUL AGENT IS THE RIGHT WORD." MARK TWAIN

There are 4 ways in which the candidate meets his voters:

1. Through personal contact. They see him at a meeting or they meet him in person—on the doorstep, in their professional organizations, in a Board of Trade meeting, or in a trade union meeting.

2. Through the media. The voter sees the candidate on television, hears him on radio, sees his picture in the newspaper, or reads what the candidate said at a meeting or interview.

3. By word of mouth, or by reputation.

4. Through material circulated by the candidate or his campaign committees. It is this subject which we are discussing now: the letter, the leaflet, the poster, the sign or billboard, and the advertisement.

THE LITERATURE CHAIRMAN As early as possible, the campaign committee should appoint a literature chairman. An experienced literature chairman has bulky files of material accumulated over the years; but here are some suggestions that show how even a beginner can get off to a flying start.

1. COLLECT MATERIAL FOR STUDY. Get a carton and place in it all the third-class mail which comes through your letter-box; ask other committee members to contribute items as well. Get samples of all your

opponent's literature. Collect old leaflets, posters, letters, and such items from previous campaigns; it may be hard to find such material when starting from scratch, but you should certainly make a point of saving it from now on. All these things are collected and preserved, not just as souvenirs, but as raw material for study. Your aim is to become an expert in this method of communicating accurate information, of arousing favourable emotions, and of stimulating people to action. Study all the examples that produced good results, and all those that failed; in each case ask why. Eventually you should be able to glance at a letter or leaflet and say, "This, this, and this are its good points, but *that* is wrong; *that* will spoil the total effect."

2. STUDY TYPOGRAPHICAL LAYOUT.   No campaign manager can go running to a professional every time a routine advertisement is placed in the local paper. So the literature chairman should know something of typographical layout. Most libraries have books on the subject. A walk down every street will show you examples, good and bad, of posters; and each one of those posters offers, in effect, a free lesson from the person who designed it. Those mass-circulation letters that you are collecting can give you ideas for designing your own circulars. Your daily newspaper offers an abundance of good advertising examples.

I have often designed display advertisements by cutting up supermarket advertisements. I turn the words upside down to render them meaningless so that I can concentrate on design. Using the letters of various sizes, I compose a simple but artistic format. First get the layout right, then add the correct copy.

3. CREATE A SLOGAN.   To express clearly and forcibly the main aspect of your broader policy you need one theme sentence or slogan. Your resources are limited; you are trying to make the maximum impact in the short time that is available during a campaign. So take pains to create a good slogan. It must be simple

and dignified, or it will not wear very well. Never forget that the key to success with posters and advertisements is to keep the message short and simple.

There is nothing wrong with issuing a leaflet that describes your program in detail, but the cover of that leaflet must sum up your program briefly and give it focus, like the cover of a book.

4. HUMANIZE YOUR MATERIAL. A good campaign is best built around the candidate. Voters are more interested in people than in programs; or at least they prefer a program to come from the lips of a human being. In his book *How To Organize an Election*, Norris Denman says, "Never sacrifice human values to administrative convenience." Remember, you are dealing with people.

Here your greatest asset is your candidate, who is carrying the message to the voter. In some elections the party label is not permitted on the ballot. If that is the case you must stress the candidate's name, because that name is the only means the voter has of recognizing your program when he goes into the voting booth.

Fortunately, Canadian federal elections now permit party labels on the ballot. It is useful to feature a reproduction of that ballot slip on some of your literature; after all, the goal of all this campaigning is getting the voter to put his X in the right place.

5. MAINTAIN UNIFORMITY. All your leaflets, posters, advertisements, and direct-mail pieces should repeat your slogan or theme sentence; all of it should bear the same symbol identifying your party; all of it that you can control should be printed in the same colour.

THE LETTER   I have always felt it necessary to send out a short letter from the candidate to the voters. This is a fairly expensive technique, but it is simple, personal, and, I believe, effective. Let us look at some variations and problems of this means of communication.

1. THE PERSONAL LETTER.   The ideal method is for the candidate to write a letter to every registered voter. He would have to wait until the voters' list is published, find a quiet place, sit down, and start writing. An assistant could fold the letters, put them in the envelopes, stick on the stamps, and mail them. That is the ideal situation and, if the constituency is small, say a thousand voters or less, it should be considered.

A telephone call from the candidate to every voter is almost as effective. A helper should look up the telephone number of every voter on the voters' list; or, if the community is small enough, the candidate can just go through the telephone book.

Because people who get a personal letter or a personal telephone call from the candidate tell their friends and neighbours, this method should be considered wherever possible. It takes less time than you would think, and it can all be done from the candidate's home.

2. THE SIMULATED PERSONAL LETTER.   Most letters from candidates to voters are simulated personal letters. A text is approved by the campaign committee and the candidate, and then the letters are reproduced by one of several processes that give varying degrees of personalization. Here are some of the methods commonly used.

(a) The letters are printed all alike, usually of 2 colours, black typewriter script on white letter-size bond paper with a second colour used to highlight the masthead and to simulate the candidate's handwriting in the signature. There need be only the 2 colours and 2 press runs. The letters are all addressed in a general manner, usually "Dear Constituent", "Dear Neighbour", "Dear Voter", or "Dear Friend", but never, please, "Dear Sir or Madam".

(b) Letters can be further personalized by leaving a blank space for the salutation at the beginning. Then you have volunteers type in the actual name and address of each voter. For this method, the printed body of the letter is set up to match the typewritten name and address. Often the same typewriter is used to prepare the photo-ready copy for the offset printing process. It takes close inspection to realize that the letter has been partly typewritten and partly printed.

Computerized typewriters can now type and sign these direct-mail letters in such a way that they are indistinguishable from an original letter, and computerized dial telephones can also call a list of voters and deliver to each a recorded message. For information on such techniques, have a talk with a direct-mail house, or with a salesman for an office-machine firm that sells or rents automated typewriter systems.

3. THE SIMPLE OFFSET PRINTED LETTER. If you do not have the time, money, or resources to produce a simulated personal letter from the candidate to the voters, the campaign committee can produce a simpler type of letter. The style and design should be just like any other pleasant, friendly, but businesslike communication. Produced by the offset photo-ready printing process, it is cheap and effective. Volunteers sign the letters on behalf of the candidate, and volunteer canvassers deliver them by hand.

In planning any of these letter formats, get lots of advice. Consult the experts. They are professional people who specialize in direct-mail techniques. Consult your printer, look at the samples that you have been saving. This is a major campaign expense, so plan every detail carefully. What colour should your envelopes be? What colour should your paper be? And, above all, keep everything simple. Your message can be deep and significant, but it must be simple, or you will not make any impression whatsoever during the election.

MAILING If you plan to use the mail for letters to voters, or for any other material, remember that the Canadian Post

Office has special regulations about mailing. Do not even order any printing until you have had a long talk with the postmaster of a large post office, and have read the special booklets which are published for the purpose of governing mass mailings.

I know one campaign manager who printed, folded, addressed, sealed, and stamped 6,000 items of mail; then the post office would not accept them because they did not meet the regulations. So, when the postmaster has agreed to your mailing program, cover the procedure with a letter from yourself to him, after the interview. Also see that the volunteers have precise written instructions for handling outgoing mail, bundling the letters according to locales, postal walks, or whatever may be required, and for delivering them to the post office.

Your postage costs can be considerably reduced if you use volunteer canvassers for delivery instead of the post office. The *Canada Elections Act*, Section 63.1, provides for compensation to candidates for the mailing and printing costs of 1 item.

THE LEAFLET   The simplest leaflet is a candidate's business card or calling card. The next simplest leaflet would be a letter from the candidate, with a printed signature, duplicated by offset in black on a white, letter-size sheet of paper, and delivered unfolded and without an envelope. It slips under doors quite easily.

A very impressive leaflet was used in the 1974 federal election which saw Ronald Basford returned for Vancouver Centre to the House of Commons, where he served for some years as Minister of Justice. His leaflet was like a minature *Life* magazine, depicting the candidate at work and play. One photograph showed Mr. Basford, his wife, and their children on the shore of Lost Lagoon in Vancouver's Stanley Park, feeding the ducks; I would have given the picture the caption "Family Neighbours". The next picture showed Mr. Basford conferring with Prime Minister Trudeau; I would have captioned that picture "With the Leader". Another photograph showed Mr.

Basford examining a magnificent wall-model of
Vancouver's reconstructed False Creek; it could have
been captioned "Leader-Planner".
Another photograph depicted Mr. Basford in short
shirtsleeves on Vancouver Centre's waterfront,
apparently explaining to a citizen and voter the
federal government's responsibility for national
harbours. The voter had his back to the camera, but
Mr. Basford was full-face. It could have been titled
"On the Job". In the final picture, the candidate was
talking to a group of senior citizens. Had I been the
campaign manager, I would have described this
picture "With Senior Citizens". The leaflet was very
effective in describing the projects in which the
Minister had been involved.

Another effective leaflet that I have seen was
mimeographed on a piece of letter-size yellow paper,
with crude, hand-lettered black figures advertising a
civic meeting. It was a throwaway meeting leaflet and
simply said "NDP Mayoralty Candidate, Tony
Gargrave, Wednesday, November 18, 12:30 Club's
Lounge, Room 212, sponsored by the University of
British Columbia NDP Club". That particular leaflet
was the perfect solution to the problem. The
university students to whom it appealed would not
have been impressed by anything more elaborate. The
leaflet was in fact used as a poster, for it was posted
on bulletin boards throughout the campus.

Do not be afraid of simplicity; do not be too
impressed by elaborate literature, but do use good
taste and good style. You must lavish just as much
care on the content and the reproduction of that
mimeographed meeting leaflet as the photographer did
on Mr. Basford's brochure.

THE POSTER   If I had to mount a campaign with only $200 to spend
on publicity, I would blow it all on a poster—one
designed so that it could be used as a poster for public
display and also as a mail-piece or a throwaway
leaflet.

The poster is one of our oldest forms of communication and is worthy of your campaign committee's time, money, and creative energy. I really think that a campaign can be built around a poster, either in the city or in the countryside.

One problem in the city is that it is difficult to get good outdoor locations for posters, so in the designing process you have to be mindful that many of them will be displayed from private homes, fastened to the inside of windows by Scotch tape. They should be fairly small, yet with colourful ink and paper so that they can be clearly seen from the street. And since you cannot tell if the posters will be used inside or outside, waterproof paper and inks should be used for all.

The timing of poster displays is worth some consideration. A voter who puts a poster in the window, or a plywood sign on the lawn, is telling the neighbours that he is committed. So if you can arrange to have all those posters appear overnight, it can have a dramatic effect on the whole constituency.

One of the most depressing sights in the world is a defeated candidate's poster, hanging at a rakish angle, with that determined smile still saying "Vote for Me". Win or lose, posters should be promptly removed after polling day.

Here is an example of poster technique from the non-political field. Every year the Vancouver Symphony Society sends a little item to each household by third-class, unaddressed, householder mail. You pick it up, folded, from the front door mat. Open it up and it turns into a magnificent, three-colour poster with portraits of Bach, Brahms, Beethoven, and Mendelssohn.

BILLBOARDS   The creative triumphs of Toulouse-Lautrec's posters of the Moulin Rouge have evolved into the monstrosities of present-day urban billboards. Yet if you have enough money, the big-city billboards can be very useful to your campaign.

If you are going to use billboards, you must prepare

early. It will be the responsibility of your literature chairman, or of your sign chairman, to get quotations and production details in time to enable your campaign committee to decide on policy and design for posters and billboards. I suggest that you get a friend to reserve billboard space in a neutral name. This way your opponents are unaware of your plans.

Bear in mind that the public will tire of seeing the same old billboard after approximately 3 months. But a simple billboard design can be freshened up in the last 21 days of a campaign by the addition of an extra dash of colour. Just adding a small paper overlay with a globe of orange on a rectangle of blue can renew the billboard's effectiveness right through to polling day.

THE LAWN SIGN   The New Democratic Party in Canada has pioneered the plywood lawn-sign, both the single-stick placard and the larger-sized variety. The latter can be seen by moving automobile traffic; it does not require professional help to make or to erect, but it does require some know-how and a lot of hard work. The usual dimensions are 1200 mm x 2400 mm (approximately 4 feet by 8 feet), the standard size in which plywood panels are sold. Background colour can be applied by anyone who can handle a paint brush; lettering is done by the silk-screen stencil process. Some technical details of this process are given later in this chapter. This silk-screening requires the supervision of a dependable member of the campaign committee.

Some election campaigns have assigned half of the campaign budget to getting these plywood signs on to constituency front lawns. The sign committee particularly attempts to place signs along main roads. Correctly located, they can have a strong psychological effect.

The plywood signs have to be affixed to posts, and a dedicated team is required to seek out locations, deliver the signs, and erect them. These signs, like the posters, should be recovered immediately after the election.

NEWSPAPER
ADVERTISING

Political advertising in the daily or weekly press falls into 3 categories.

1. Message advertising, containing a considerable amount of explanatory material on policy or program. These are sometimes described as "reader ads"; they may contain as many as 300 words. Strong constituencies purchase message ads for the ethnic and vocational press.

2. Institutional or display advertising, which is just showing the flag, as with "Support Our Party", "Vote for Me", or some such exhortation. National and provincial parties have to do a minimum amount of this display advertising as a support to their struggling individual candidates. Head offices are aware that certain constituencies are weak, so newspaper advertising helps paper over the cracks and provides a semblance of a campaign in throwaway ridings. This showing of the flag is essential; you must not let your opponents buy all the display space. Your party should have some of the action.

3. Specific-event advertising, in which you invite the public to attend a meeting, a dinner, or a coffee party.

In my provincial election experience, my advertising in the daily and weekly press was restricted to Category 3, advertising meetings, and then, in the last week of a campaign I added some Category 2 messages.

I rarely used the press to sell my program; I was concerned with the constituency level rather than the national or provincial campaign and felt that leaflets were more effective.

Here are 2 important points regarding newspaper advertising.

1. Where a number of people are running for public office on the same ballot, and the public needs to remember a list of names, that list or slate must be advertised in the papers 3 or 4 days before the election, so that voters can clip the ad and take it to the polls.

2. If you have lots of money, be careful not to overadvertise. If you spend money like a drunken sailor, people become suspicious of your judgment and your activities. It seems likely that, in the future, there are going to be increasing restrictions on campaign expenditures through legislation which will require campaign managers to be more careful in the spending of donated funds.

See Section 61.2 of the *Canada Elections Act* for restrictions on advertising.

MAKING SILK-
SCREEN SIGNS

Silk-screen printing is a stencilling process that is fairly cheap, easy to use, and very versatile. With silk-screening you can produce all kinds of signs, posters, bumper-stickers, and other useful campaign material. Imaginative friends will be able to do creative things with silk-screening, but here I would recommend, as in other aspects of campaigning, that you keep it simple.

Now for a few technical details. The stencil, nowadays more likely to be of nylon than of silk, is stretched taut on a wooden frame, something like a big picture frame. The stencil is covered with a wax coating, called profilm, which is impervious to the ink. Wherever you cut away this profilm, the ink will go through.

Once the system is in operation, you can silk-screen on paper, card, or plywood, depending on your requirements. You lift the frame that carries the stencil, place the material to be printed on a flat, smooth table, lower your frame, pour on the ink, and squeeze the ink through the cut-away lettering or other design on the stencil. Then you lift the screen, remove the newly stencilled sign, put in a new sheet of paper, lower the frame again, and so on.

If your stencil is professionally cut, you can do an impressive reproduction job. Once the process is in operation, any walk-in volunteer can operate the system with ten minutes' instruction and some supervision.

It is essential to have good-quality materials if you are seeking good results. Hunt up the nearest supplier in your locality for the screen, profilm, paints, or inks. Silk-screen inks should be kept warm prior to mixing. They must also be diluted with a light solvent, such as Varsol, to the point at which it passes easily through the screen stencil.

It is important to choose the right colours for your inks. If you are the sign chairman, check with party headquarters to find out the shade that they recommend and ask advice on the actual brand and number of the oil paint and printer's ink. There is a lot of difference between robin's-egg blue, lavender blue, and dark navy-blue. Colours used for this work should be standard right across the nation, right down to catalogue ordering-numbers; so insist that printers and volunteers use this identical colour.

For paper signs, you can keep the white background and stencil the message in your party colour. For the 1200 mm x 2400 mm plywood signs you can use the party colour as a base, applied with a brush all over the panel: the message is then stencilled over this background in black or some strongly contrasting colour. You might reinforce the concept of victory at the polls with a simple ballot-like design such as:

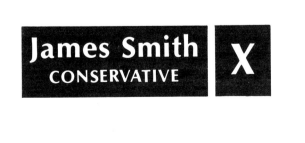

One more piece of equipment is needed—a squeegee to spread the ink over the screen. Squeegees can be purchased by the inch, so buy one exactly big enough to fit inside the screen you are using; this allows you to print your sign with one or two strokes.

An important part of producing professional-looking signs and posters from the silk-screen process is keeping the screen clean. You must never allow ink to dry on the stencil, so when you finish the day's work, the screen must be cleaned. Do not use lacquer thinner to clean your screen, because it dissolves the wax profilm.

This silk-screening is simple but messy. So, unless you have a very big committee room, you will need a special location for your silk-screening. Sign production and distribution is a great volunteer project, and an amazing *esprit de corps* can be created. Make your plans well in advance and build up your stocks of paint, lumber, paper, and plywood. With a bit of luck, you will be able to locate the sign chairman from the last election and re-energize his old crew.

Put a few signs out early in the campaign, but go right ahead with the production so that, as I mentioned before, you can put a whole lot of them up on the same day, to create that psychological peak during the last lap of the campaign. But keep some sign capacity in reserve, in case there is a serious attempt to deface or remove all your signs. Do not damage or remove your opponent's signs. If there is a problem with removal or damage of signs in your constituency, persuade all the parties to form a little committee and approach the police chief about it. You can create a nice little news story out of the incident, and perhaps the news photographer will choose your sign as an illustration.

An integral part of your planning will be for the retrieval of all signs after the election and the safe storage of all materials until next time.

During the 1970 Vancouver civic election, it was necessary to prepare signs for the whole city, and we set up a sign shop in an abandoned church on Venables Street in Vancouver's east end. We were running a total civic slate of twenty-five members, and we insisted that every candidate, including the mayoralty candidate, spend one full evening at the sign shop.

PHOTOGRAPHS   No chapter on campaign literature can be complete without some discussion of photography. A closely framed, head-and-shoulders, two-ear picture of the candidate against a neutral background is often chosen to depict the candidate, and hence to project the party and the election policy. To get even such a basic photo may not be as simple as it sounds. In 1949, in one of the earliest federal elections I was involved in, a last-minute scramble for photos produced a portrait of the candidate without a tie. The campaign committee solemnly declared that a tie was required, and an artist sketched in a tie over the glossy black-and-white positive.

If the candidate turns one-quarter to the left or to the right, as his political views dictate, you end up with a head-and-shoulder, one-ear picture. Some years ago, Mr. Ralph Campney, MP, Minister of Defence, instructed all military establishments to replace his dour two-ear, head-and-shoulders picture with a smiling one-ear picture. The House of Commons had some fun with the military memorandum when it turned up in debate.

A popular variation is to show the candidate with gesturing hand, speaking into a microphone (which should be slightly below his chin) or talking on the phone. Some candidates seem to have telephones glued permanently to their left ears.

A good photographer can tell something about the candidate's character or background with his pictures. Placing the candidate in front of an aircraft reminds voters that he is a distinguished pilot. Depicting the candidate against a well-filled bookcase is a reminder of his academic background. A photo of the candidate with spouse and children against some recognizable local landmark shows him as a solid citizen. Photographs of the candidate canvassing, shaking hands, making a speech, nailing up a poster, and so on, show him as a vigorous campaigner.

A photograph can tell a story. If you are fortunate enough to have as a candidate an incumbent in a legislative or municipal council, you might consider these photographic stories:

1. Member visiting with constituents in the parliamentary restaurant.
2. Member doing research in the library, standing alongside a card-file with the drawer open.
3. Member conversing with the Speaker or Clerk, who is wearing full regalia.
4. Member speaking to constituents or to the party leader on the front steps of the legislature.
5. Member conversing with the leader in an office or interior setting.
6. Member dictating a letter to a stenographer.
7. Member attending caucus or committee meeting.
8. Member entering or leaving the main exterior door of City Hall.
9. Member talking to the press.
10. Member outside a committee room or council chamber, showing the wording on the door.
11. Member in his seat in the legislative chamber or council, signing a letter or conversing with a nearby member.
12. Member examining a vertical map or graph.
13. Member with his family against the legislative buildings.
14. Member consulting papers, making a speech, casting a ballot, or any other action associated with his office.

If you are the campaign manager or literature chairman, you should save, or arrange for, all the photographs you can get. But you should have only good photographs: throw out all those that are second-rate—those with fuzzy or cluttered backgrounds, and those with microphones hiding the candidate's mouth and nose or lampposts growing out of the top of the candidate's head. Study good photographs; get the advice of press photographers and layout technicians. Ask yourself, "What does this picture say?" and "What can this picture do?" Ask around: if seven out of ten people say they do not like a picture, do not use it.

Use photographs according to your budget. If funds are limited, you may wish to make do with a pleasant passport snapshot, or you may decide to invest all your money in 1 leaflet and 1 creative photograph.

Remember, too, that the most judicious selection process will be fruitless unless your photographs are well reproduced. In one city campaign in which I participated, we printed 100,000 copies of a 2-colour brochure in which the front picture was indecipherable because of a poor background and clumsy overprinting. That photograph contributed little to the leaflet or the campaign.

MOVIES   Colour and sound movie-film, carefully edited, is the best visual medium for projecting the candidate and his policy in the precious seconds of TV time. For example, if you want to talk about harbour policy for your city, take the candidate down to the harbour and let him explain his policy in full view of the white-flecked green waves, the blue sky, and the warm, orange sun. Remember to always treat the voter as an adult; do not talk down to him.

LEAFLET   1. Define campaign focus: candidate, policy, or
PLANNING   party.
CHECKLIST   2. Decide purpose, sequence, and priority of leaflets
               for the following:
               (a) leaflet for first canvass   ☐
               (b) leaflet for second general canvass   ☐
               (c) leaflet for candidate's canvass   ☐
               (d) leaflet for ethnic canvass   ☐
               (e) leaflet for special vocation canvass   ☐

LEAFLET DESIGN
CHECKLIST

For each leaflet to be used, check these items:

1. Find out postal regulations. ☐
2. Design basic layout, including attention-getting cover and photos if required. ☐
3. Write text for leaflet, captions for pictures. Do not crowd your copy. Do not needlessly vary typefaces. ☐
4. Publisher's name must appear on leaflet (*Canada Elections Act*, Section 72). ☐
5. Place union symbol on literature. ☐
6. Place telephone number and address of committee room on all literature. ☐
7. Use sparse colour for emphasis. ☐
8. Plan to use standard paper sizes for economy. ☐
9. Draw the "dummy" to instruct the printer. ☐

LEAFLET
PRODUCTION
CHECKLIST

1. Find a good printer who will give sound advice and who will carry out instructions. ☐
2. Ascertain paper-stock sizes, availability, and waterproof qualities. ☐
3. Check correct colour and availability of your party ink. ☐
4. Check available typeface. ☐
5. Proofread material carefully. Use 2 proofreaders, both of them to sign the copy. ☐

PHOTO
CHECKLIST

Choose photographs required:

(a) head and shoulders ☐
(b) character ☐
(c) issue or policy ☐
(d) story ☐
(e) campaigning ☐
(f) family ☐

The
News Media

YOU CAN BE NEWSWORTHY BY SHOOTING YOUR
CAMPAIGN MANAGER.

Many candidates fail to use the news media properly. Then when they do not get the coverage they would like, they feel that there is a conspiracy of reporters, photographers, editors, and publishers to ignore them and to publicize other candidates.

This is not true. Failure to get news coverage stems from failure on the candidate's part to qualify for it. The editors and producers of newspapers, magazines, radio, and TV need and want relevant news. There are 2 sure steps to getting good coverage:

1. Say and do things that are newsworthy.

2. Make sure that the news media know what you have said and done.

WHAT IS NEWS?   News is information that is new to the person who is receiving it. But newness is not enough to qualify material as newsworthy.

Here are some ways in which you can make a piece of information newsworthy in the eyes of the media and the general public.

1. You must be *innovative*. You must do and say old truths in new ways.

2. The more directly the information concerns the public to whom it is addressed the better. Most people welcome the chance of talking to a candidate. They may have questions they wish to ask or they may just be excited by the prospect of

being photographed, or of getting on TV, while being in conversation with the candidate. This element of *personal concern* is essential.

3. The more *conflict* your information contains, the better.

Conflict is the prime ingredient for arousing interest in stories, books, plays, films, and sport. Conflict is the main source of interest in poker, bridge, billiards, chess, or darts—conflict between individuals or teams to see who will win. The same principle holds good in the presentation of news: the stronger the conflict and the more interesting the item, the more likely it is to be used, to be noticed, to be remembered.

So, do not just state what your policy is on a certain issue: also say who or what is the opposition to your policy, why they are wrong, and just how you propose to defeat them if you get the chance. *That's conflict!*

Do not say that candidate Joe Smith expects an easy victory in the election: little conflict means little news value. Say that he is conducting an all-out struggle against a well-financed opposition.

These days there is no point pretending that raising campaign funds for elections is easy. In fact, it is a hard struggle, a conflict. A good news story is to tell the world how much you are going to spend and just how you are going to raise that money.

Your main conflict will normally be with your individual opponents, and also with the parties they represent, especially with the government, if you are not in power. Keep on looking for new elements of conflict; keep on hammering at them in all your publicity. It's the key to creating news.

Heavyweight boxer Muhammad Ali demonstrates great skill at whipping up conflict in advance of his fights, and in making them newsworthy.

4. The stronger the element of *suspense* your information contains, the better. A good, sus-

penseful story interests the reader today, and also sets him wondering how something is going to turn out in the future.

Suppose Joe Smith says, "I'm not yet satisfied that we fully know what is bothering the voters of this constituency. I shall be keeping a tally of the points that people raise with me at my morning public interviews, and each day I shall release the totals, with my comments on what they signify and my proposals as to what should be done about them."

Here he has created suspense. Some people, at least, will be wondering what results the informal survey will yield; some of the media people will come back to the candidate for the up-to-date totals and his comments upon them.

Many media people appreciate the value of suspense, as long as the story is genuinely about new, conflict-laden material.

It sometimes becomes difficult to get news into the daily papers during the closing days of an election campaign. Editors may feel that readers are getting tired of your candidate; there may be strong competition from other candidates for the available space. Still, you cannot afford to give up. At this stage you should make special effort to aim for something novel in the news that you are creating. Do not put all your efforts into your own campaign meetings; it can be very useful to get your candidate on the platform at the regular meetings of other community groups, as sole speaker or as part of a debate. An alert campaign manager will be on the lookout for taxpayers' meetings, university lunch-hour meetings, and professional and union groups that might like a speaker. These platforms assist you in getting news coverage.

You cannot expect all your press releases to be published on Page One. My own press releases have often seen the light of day following the classified ads; but I was glad to get the coverage.

LETTERS TO THE
EDITOR

Nearly every newspaper and magazine has a "letters-to-the-editor" section. This publicity channel is not used as it might be. When an election campaign is in full swing, some papers will not publish letters that are obvious plugs for one of the candidates. Nevertheless, this section can still be useful.

1. I have mentioned elsewhere the advantages of an early start for a campaign—months or years ahead of the election. As soon as your candidate is nominated, he can start writing letters to the editor. A good strategy is to select a few subjects—preferably those on which he is specially qualified—and appoint himself as general critic on those subjects.

A good letter to the editor for this purpose:

(a) Is "pegged" to some contentious topical issue.

(b) Is fact-filled and relevant.

(c) Clearly reveals the candidate's knowledge of the subject.

(d) Offers solutions.

(e) Is short and pithy (about 150 words) and is neatly typed.

2. For someone who already holds office, letters to the editor are a good means of keeping oneself before the eye of the voter back home, and of preparing the ground for the next election.

3. During a campaign, when letters from candidates are not being accepted, you can get supporters to write to the papers.

Letters to the editor can also be a first-class means of obtaining information. Any candidate for office should want to know as much as possible about his constituency and its affairs, past and present; but many important, interesting pieces of local history, ancient or recent, have never been put down in books. A good way to find out about them is to write a letter to the editor asking if there is anyone who has the particular bit of knowledge you are seeking. Explain why you want it. You will, of course, reply personally to anyone who writes to you, and, if you do get the required information, send a follow-up

letter to the editor, reporting your success and
thanking him.

This sort of quest is useful in itself, and is also an
excellent means of building goodwill: many people
feel well-disposed towards a candidate who shows
that he is willing to learn. Moreover, the people who
have given you information become your friends:
they will enjoy telling others how they helped the
candidate or the member.

PRESS RELEASES   Films and TV shows often portray a candidate
surrounded by hard-driving reporters, who are
bombarding him with questions, and the answers he
gives become front-page stories with huge headlines.
In reality, interviews are only a part of a candidate's
dealings with the news media: a lot of what he has to
communicate goes by way of press releases.

The press release is a specialized form of pro-
motion: wrongly produced, it will simply waste
your time and money; used well, it will efficiently
convey your message, and will earn you the goodwill
of the news-media people.

This subject is so important that I am going to
cover it in some detail.

THE INVERTED   Every news story has to be in a special format,
PYRAMID   because the reporter who writes it does not know how
much of it the editor is going to use. It is quite likely
that the editor will not be able to use it all, but as he
has no time to shorten or rewrite the story he will
simply cut off as much as is necessary to make it fit
the available space. Now, whether 5 percent or 65
percent of the original is cut, the part that remains
must seem complete and coherent. News, therefore, is
written in the so-called "inverted pyramid" format.

The whole story is summed up in the first sentence;
additional details follow, arranged in descending order
of importance.

There is another reason for using the inverted
pyramid. Not many newspaper readers have time to
read the whole paper through; so they can skim the

most important parts of the news by reading just the first few lines of each story.

Read the papers carefully, until you can spot this formula in action, can discern the various sections of each news story, and can see the reasons why each item is placed where it is. The inverted pyramid does not apply to editorials and feature articles: here the writer knows exactly how long his article must be, and will often leave some of his most interesting material for the very end.

But a press release is meant to provide news; so every press release must be written in the inverted pyramid.

THE LEAD

The first, biggest, most important element of your pyramid is called the lead. The quality of your lead determines whether the editor throws your release straight into the wastebasket, or whether he reads further, and perhaps uses it. If the story is used, the quality of your lead determines how much of it the general reader will read.

Your lead should tell who did what, when, and where, and also, if the information is relevant, why and how.

BE EXACT

In the lead, and right through the story, all your facts should be *exact*. For example, it is inadequate to say that the candidate is a "big man"; say instead that he stands 6 feet 3 inches in his shoes, and weighs 211 pounds without a topcoat. It is not sufficient to write about a "large audience"; one reader might think a hundred was large; another might think two hundred was small. It is better to say that every chair in the 460-seat auditorium was filled, and fifteen people were standing.

FORMAT

1. A press release must be typed, double spaced or triple spaced, on letter-size paper, 8½″ x 11″. Use

pica or elite type; there is a prejudice against italic, gothic, script, or other fancy typefaces.

2. To avoid any possible confusion with a letter to the editor, it is customary to type the words PRESS RELEASE at the top of the sheet.

3. The name, address, and telephone number of the candidate, campaign manager, and organization come next.

4. Sometimes it is necessary to delay use of the material until a certain time. If so, put a notification of the date and hour, in this form: "For release June 5, 1976, 12 noon". If the material is for use at once, put "For Immediate Release".

5. Next comes the message; 250 words is about the right length. Do not give your release a headline. Editors like to write their own headlines, and many of them resent it if someone else tries to do the job for them. The conventional mark for the end of the message is -30-.

Here, as an example, is one of my own press releases:

PRESS RELEASE

Tony Gargrave
Parliament Buildings
Victoria, B.C. —

Tel: 382-6111

January 27, 1966.

A strong drive for complete rebuilding and reorganization of the Sechelt Peninsular highway to 50 mph standards, will be advocated on the floor of the Legislature which opened recently in Victoria.

Tony Gargrave, MLA, said that the rebuilding of this highway would cut travel time from Powell River to Vancouver to four hours. "This four-hour travel time, based on two-hour ferry schedules, plus later evening trips on the Langdale-Horseshoe Bay run, would solve some of the delays on this route," Gargrave said.

The local MLA envisioned a new location for the Peninsular Highway 101 that avoided schools and communities with feeder routes into the new highway. "The existing road should be improved for local traffic," he said.

-30-

And here is a newspaper story that resulted from this press release.

BETTER HIGHWAY IS MLA'S AIM

A strong drive for the complete rebuilding and relocation of the Sechelt Peninsula Highway to 50 mph standards will be advocated on the floor of the legislature opening Thursday in Victoria. Tony Gargrave, Mackenzie riding MLA, said that the rebuilding of this highway would cut travel time from Powell River to Vancouver to four hours. The trip takes about 5½ hours now. This four-hour travel time, based on ferries every two hours, plus later evening trips on the Langdale-Horseshoe Bay run, would solve some of the delays on this route, Gargrave said.

Gargrave envisioned a new location for Peninsula Highway 101, that avoided schools and communities.

The existing road should be improved for local traffic with feeder routes into the new highway, he suggested.

(Jan. 27/76 PR NEWS)

GETTING IT IN   Find out what the deadlines are for the various media, and make sure that your material gets in ahead of time.

Material that goes in late might as well not be sent at all. This point cannot be overstressed. Do not hesitate to use the telephone, telegraph, telex, taxicab, or special delivery, to get your material in to the papers or other news services on time.

The campaign manager and the candidate should make an appointment with the news editor of each outlet, right at the start of the campaign, to talk about the campaign and, if possible, to get introductions to the reporter or reporters who will be covering it. Ask the editor how *he* wants the news to come in.

Do not forget the weekly press; provide them with news stories, biographies, and pictures.

Do not forget the wire services. Canadian Press may put your story on the news wire, which reaches almost every news outlet in the country, including radio and television.

THE BROADCAST MEDIA   Nowadays radio and television are probably the most powerful means of campaigning: through radio and TV you can reach people who do not attend public meetings, who do not read newspapers, and who would certainly never think of joining a political party.

Radio and TV time is much easier to get than it used to be, particularly in smaller communities. Local radio and TV stations want to cover local events, and elections may be expected to provide some good news-coverage.

But it's not all as easy as it seems. A beginner may find broadcasting confusing, even frightening, at first. On radio the speaker may be shut up alone, inside a small, dimly lit, and acoustically dead studio; there, with only a microphone to talk to, he must try to project a warm, friendly, outgoing personality to thousands of people working in kitchens, driving automobiles, or lying on beaches. In a TV studio, he will be surrounded by blazing lights, shifting cameras, and a platoon of personnel; here he must attend to the director's signals, and simultaneously must seem to be concentrating on answering the questions of an interviewer or on debating with other members of a panel.

PLAY IT SAFE   In selecting a candidate for an election, you must decide whether he can do a good job of presenting your platform and policies on radio and television, as well as in public meetings and in print. On television your candidate will be judged by his appearance, on radio by the sound of his voice. You should consider the same thing in assessing your own chance as a candidate in an election. It may not be fair; it may not be your idea of true democracy; but it is a fact that these qualities are vital to the success of any campaign.

Here are some suggestions about what to do if the candidate is not up to scratch in this department.

1. If you have sufficient time, you may be able to arrange for the candidate to be coached in radio and television performance. Some night schools offer such courses; some community radio and TV stations have programs where beginners can get experience. This is yet another good reason for starting your campaign far in advance of the election call.

2. If the candidate's only weakness is that he comes over badly on television, it may be a good idea to let someone else do the TV work for him. There need be no feeling of embarrassment. It's the same as having someone else write the press releases or design the posters.

3. An inexperienced candidate can minimize the risks inherent in broadcasting by being brief and simple. A snappy 2-minute or 3-minute talk or interview is not likely to do much harm, and the curiosity value of the fresh face and voice will help to keep the public interested. But a bad 10-minute performance could injure the campaign. So, if in doubt, get on and off quickly.

Now for some specific technical points.

THE PERSONAL TOUCH   For radio and television alike, one important point must be stressed: the style of speaking is not oratorical, but conversational. You may be addressing thousands of people, but they are not a crowd. They have not come out to a meeting to hear you deliver a speech: they have permitted you to come into their homes, as a visitor, and they can get rid of you by flipping a switch. The rule, then, for broadcasting, must be an easy, courteous, personal approach. Know your material well, so that you can relax while talking.

An exception is when a radio or TV broadcast is made of an actual public meeting. The speaker then uses an ordinary platform technique, for the sake of the live audience in the hall. The broadcast audience will understand the situation.

RADIO Now that television is with us, many candidates look down their noses at radio. But every medium has to be evaluated in terms of its cost and its effectiveness. A simple black-and-white leaflet may not be as effective as a colour one, but, on the other hand, if it is all that you can afford, it is better than nothing.

You should also keep in mind that you can get a spot on radio quickly; in the event of suddenly emerging issues on which you wish to speak, this can be very useful. And the production costs are low. If your riding is a rural one and television reception is poor or nonexistent, you may wish to use radio.

If you are operating in a large city, you can use the radio to go on record on a particular issue. Or, you may wish to bounce a press release off a radio audience; after the radio address, you can issue a press release to the other media.

Radio can also be a convenient way in which to report to your constituents. You may have just come back from the legislature, or from a significant trip abroad, and wish to bring your constituents up to date. Radio is a quick way of telling interested people what you have done or what you intend to do. And unlike a meeting, a radio broadcast cannot fail because of poor attendance.

Occasionally I would report to my constituents through radio. This is the way I went about it. I booked my time on the radio station that I believed would reach the greatest number of my constituents. A radio station will always advise you of its listening area. I then decided what I wanted to say and how long I would speak. Before the broadcast, I booked advertising space in the weekly newspapers in the area so that my constituents would know of the broadcast. And the fact that people did not listen did not really matter because they would see the advertising and approve, even if they did not listen. In other words, they were invited but could not come, but were pleased to be invited. I also mailed a chatty letter, black on white with a blue signature, advising my constitutents of legislative matters in general and the radio broadcast in particular. It was sent in a "sealed-yet-open" envelope, therefore getting the lowest printed householder rate. You do not have to address householder mail. On the outside of the envelope was printed an advertisement for the radio program, and it was mailed to every household in the area. Total costs were about $600. The 3-way approach of radio, householder mail, and weekly newspaper advertisements could not fail to have an impact on the household of almost every voter. The folding and stuffing of the envelopes was done by volunteer labour.

The weekly newspapers ran a little news story informing readers of the coming broadcast. After the broadcast, we issued a news release to the same newspapers, advising them of the contents of the radio broadcast. This created a new story the following week.

Radio enables you to get more factual content into your talk than television. It is easier and less expensive to stage a radio broadcast than a public meeting. Although radio does not have the emotional impact of colour television, it does allow the candidate to deal with straight factual matters quickly, and it can be pre-recorded and broadcast at a convenient time. So, all in all, radio in the right place at the right time can be an efficient election weapon. Preparation need not be elaborate, though it must be done properly. Here are some technical hints.

1. VOICE QUALITY.   The typical small radio receiver in home or automobile tends to make the human voice sound thin and tinny. A partial remedy for this is to pitch your voice down towards the lower portion of your range—women towards the contralto, men towards the bass. Also, on radio you have no facial expressions or hand gestures to add interest, so it is important to use more than your normal variety of pace, power, and pitch. But be careful not to go high and squeaky! It is also good to make yourself use a variety of facial expressions; these changes can't be seen, but they do produce perceptible changes in the tonal quality of your voice. Clarity is important, too; so take special care to articulate distinctly.

2. SIMPLICITY.   Many listeners are not concentrating on the radio; they are using it as a background to housework, driving, woodcarving, knitting, eating, drinking, talking, or what-have-you. So your message must be simple, straightforward, clear, if it is to capture their attention. Radio scripts and radio talks are not the place for elegant style, complex arguments, and recondite allusions. "Recondite allusions", for example, would be a bad phrase for radio.

3. PAID SPOT-ANNOUNCEMENTS.   These may be useful if you can afford them. In small, one-radio-station towns they can be cheap and effective. The script is carefully prepared in advance, and usually has to be checked by the station management for length and content, because there are regulations on the use of paid political announcements in an election campaign. This sort of announcement can be compared with a cheerful, warm telegram that will give your message in 50 seconds of reading time. Test the text on the campaign committee first. Rely on their gut reaction to your material and delivery style. Do not use untested material.

I like to hear a candidate read his own spot commercials. You do not want them to sound as if you are reading off a script, but you do wish to sound authoritative. Practise with a tape recorder and one or two discriminating advisers before going to the station for the actual recording. If your advisers tell you that you do not read well, have a professional announcer do it for you. Do not drive the voters away with an unpleasant accent or halting delivery.

4. TALK SHOWS.　A favourite radio technique is the talk show; the host has you in for 20 minutes or so to talk about the campaign. These shows should not be difficult, for the interviewers are generally adept at keeping the conversation going. Talk as you would to a neighbour; be frank and modest, but speak with authority. One caution: this type of performance is supposed to be a *conversation*, so do not hog the show, do not go on too long without a pause: frame your remarks to give the interviewer natural, easy openings for comments and questions.

5. PHONE-IN SHOWS.　Here you will almost certainly run into some criticism and opposition. This can be dealt with politely, much as you would handle similar questions at a public meeting or in your home. Be patient and do not get angry. You can kick your campaign manager later, but do not put down the obnoxious listener with a sharp reply.

TELEVISION　1. APPEARANCE.　Television tends to exaggerate some features of one's appearance. Fat people look fatter, a man's beard-shadow looks darker, and jewellery looks brighter. The general rule, then, is to aim for moderation. Men should wear single-colour suits of medium-dark colour and pastel single-coloured shirts —not white; wear long socks so that when you sit down you will not show an expanse of bare ankle and droopy hose. It can have a near-hypnotic effect, drawing a viewer's eyes away from your face! Avoid wristwatches with brilliantly reflective cases or hands. If you usually shave, shave carefully as close as possible to showtime. The studio people may still

decide to apply some make-up to your face. A suntan
helps. Sit in front of a sunlamp for a few minutes a
day.

Women should wear plain clothes in pastel colours
(no hats, no brilliant jewellery) and ordinary street
make-up. If you generally wear glasses, keep them on
for television.

Always check your appearance carefully in a mirror
before entering the studio; it will give you more
confidence on camera. Never arrive late. It will make
you nervous.

2. VOICE QUALITY.   Because the sound system of the
typical TV receiver is better than that of the ordinary
home radio, and because you can rely on your facial
expression to help put your message across, you do
not need to work quite so hard on vocal variety. Just
maintain a clear, pleasant conversational style.

3. BEHAVIOUR.   As on radio, bear in mind that the
medium is bringing you into the living rooms of the
audience. One difference from radio, though, is that
most TV viewers are probably paying fairly close
attention to the program: that makes your task
somewhat easier.

Your posture helps to create the viewer's impression
of your personality. Do not slump; do not lean back.
If possible, sit in a chair that helps to keep you
upright. If you must use a low chair or couch, lean
forward rather than back. Get to the studio early and
have a chat with the producer.

Often you cannot tell what image the viewers are
seeing on their television set. For example, an
interviewer may be asking a question, or another
guest may be making a statement, while a camera
picks up your reaction to it. So do not risk being
caught picking your nose, scratching your head, or
yawning. You should sit still and look at the person
who is speaking.

A special point about the ending of a TV show:
after the program seems to be over, do not jump up

and start taking off the clip-on microphone, or make such remarks as, "Well, that went better than I expected." Perhaps a picture from the studio is being superimposed over the closing titles of the show, or perhaps the sound has not been turned off. Stay where you are, look pleasant, and say nothing until you are told to move.

4. PAID ANNOUNCEMENT. These are much more expensive than radio spots, and filming or videotaping is so difficult that it can only be done by people who have the technical knowledge. If you are going to buy TV time and professional production skills, be sure to get good value.

Do not simply have the candidate stand before the camera and talk; television viewers are accustomed to visual variety and will quickly become bored. By all means begin and end on the candidate, but consider what other material can be used in between: still photos, segments of film or videotape, exhibits, or a map.

The candidate does not need to talk all the time. Consider using short segments of appropriate sound effects, such as traffic noises, children playing, or the applause of an audience.

5. TALKS AND INTERVIEWS. Here, too, bear in mind the advantage of visual variety, and take any opportunity to show photos and exhibits. Mention your plans to the producer in advance, and he or his assistant will help you do display them. Consider using a black-board; but if you do, make sure any figures or diagrams you draw are legible to the audience. If you are using notes, or reading the occasional passage from a script, do not try to conceal the fact. The audience will not mind, so long as you do not gaze down at the paper too often or too long.

Douglas Fisher, MP, was elected by going on TV once a week in Thunder Bay, Ontario. With a blackboard and a piece of chalk, he gave his con-stituents little lectures on political reality. He was a political unknown, but his TV audience loved it, and he was elected with a landslide. Television was new in those days.

6. OBSERVATION. As soon as you start planning to use television for your campaign, observe carefully how other people use the medium. You will probably see some bad examples; analyse them, find out exactly what you do not like, and be forewarned. You will also see some first-class examples; here too, analyse, learn, and be guided accordingly.

MEDIA
RELATIONS
So much for the specific techniques of the various news media; now for some general thoughts on building good relationships with them.

You might start your campaign by putting on a lunch for the candidate, the campaign committee, and the media representatives. Invite:

(a) Daily newspapers
(b) Weekly papers
(c) Ethnic press
(d) Union and professional press
(e) Television
(f) Radio

Each person should receive a personally signed invitation from the candidate. It creates a better impression in the mind of the recipient than a duplicated notice would. The invitation should give the names, addresses, and telephone numbers of the campaign manager and the candidate. The news editors will file them for future reference.

Even if some of these people cannot come, they appreciate the polite invitation, and they will know that your campaign is alive and well.

Do not overdo the hospitality: a simple lunch in a quiet place is sufficient. Have a press release ready to give them. Discuss your campaign plans, and do not hesitate to ask the media people how they would like to receive the news. They are in the business of gathering and publishing news, and it is to the mutual advantage of candidate and newsman that the news comes in. Whether they will publish *your* news depends entirely on the news value of your material, and on your credibility as a candidate.

One way to break into an afternoon paper is to get up at 5 a.m., pick up the morning paper off your front porch, and read it from cover to cover. Then telephone the afternoon paper and tell them that you have a comment on a certain news story in the morning paper. If you are lucky, the city editor will say, "Thank goodness you phoned. I've got to rewrite that morning paper story, and it needs a fresh slant."

I have mentioned some of the difficulties of using radio and television. Yet bear in mind that the people who work in these media have a personal and professional interest in putting out high-quality shows. There are lots of good people in the business who, even if they would not vote for you, will help you with your radio or television technique. If you need technical advice, *do not be afraid to ask*, well in advance, when the broadcast is first scheduled. It may be possible to arrange a rehearsal or a practice session, during which the speaker can get acquainted with the physical set-up, and can be given some practical hints on improving his performance. Here again, a little effort spent on creating good relations will result in improved news coverage.

TIPS ON
EFFECTIVE USE
OF THE MEDIA

NEWSPAPER ADVERTISING

Get to know
1. Salesmen
2. Rates
3. Datelines

Basic Rules
1. Use lots of white space.
2. Include an action picture of the candidate.
3. Have a catching and imaginative headline.
4. During last few weeks place ads in:
   dailies (last week)
   weeklies (last 2 weeks).
5. Always include telephone number and address.

6. Ask for election support as well as vote.
7. Include authorization or name of publisher.

RADIO COMMERCIALS

Get to know
1. Key personnel and production people
2. Rates and key listening-hours
3. Deadlines
4. Listening areas

Basic Rules
1. Aim commercials as to time and content at your greatest support.
2. Keep commercials brief—10- or 60-second spots. Use 1 idea per announcement.
3. Do not say too much. The listener can only absorb so much at one time.
4. Start with an attention-getting statement.
5. Repeat an idea several times.
6. Use your candidate if he has a good radio voice.

TELEVISION

You should
1. Use professional help.
2. Get facts on cost and coverage.
3. Speak to individual viewers.
4. Use 30- or 60-second spots.

Political Surveys

Political surveys are being used more and more to assess the views of the electorate. In the 1968 U.S. presidential election campaign, Richard Nixon's Washington campaign headquarters could poll the whole of the United States in one day by the use of Wide Area Telephone Service. This system enabled a switchboard in Washington to phone a controlled sample anywhere in the country. Before the end of the day the presidential candidate knew how the people of the United States felt about any particular issue—at least, how those who had telephones felt.

I think that any well-run campaign requires at least some minimal polling on political attitudes. Guessing on these questions is not good enough. Even careful debate by candidates and policy committees is not good enough, unless it is based upon knowledge of the facts. Stephen Shadegg, author of *How to Win an Election*, got fed up with people coming to his state of Arizona, saying, "Well, I expect you want me to talk about water conservation." Shadegg said that, in fact, people did not want to hear about water conservation, and that what politicians think are hot issues may not be hot issues at all.

A candidate who knows what his electorate is thinking has a tremendous advantage over a candidate who is battling, electorally, in the dark. Opinion-surveying could scarcely be called simple, but it is certainly no mystery: a dozen intelligent men and women who want to help a particular candidate could do him a tremendous service by running political-attitude surveys.

LEGAL RESTRICTIONS   Some electoral jurisdictions have laws against taking straw votes once the election is called. For example, Section 166 of the B.C. *Provincial Elections Act* says,

No person, corporation or organization shall, after the issue of the writ for any election, take any straw vote which will, prior to the election, distinguish the political opinions of the voters in any electoral district.

In a recent provincial election in British Columbia, a local hamburger-seller offered three kinds of hamburgers—a Bennettburger, a Barrettburger, and a McGeerburger—named after the leaders of the three political parties contesting the election. He reported daily to the press on the sales of the three varieties, and correctly forecast the victory of Premier W. A. C. Bennett. In British Columbia, after the election writ was issued, this "straw vote" was clearly illegal.

However, I do not think there is any objection to taking political-attitude surveys on issues, rather than on candidates or political parties, while an election campaign is on. But the most effective polls are taken before the election writ is issued.

INFORMAL SAMPLING   There are several ways of taking informal information surveys without having any separate organization, volunteer or professional, set up for the purpose.

1. LETTER-WRITING.   You can send to each of your supporters a letter enclosing 2 copies of a questionnaire. You ask the supporter to fill in 1 questionnaire himself, to call on 1 person of opposite political beliefs with the second copy, and then to return both of them to the candidate by mail.

2. TELEPHONING. If I was a member of a parliamentary caucus, I would arrange for each member's secretary to phone 50 representative people in the constituency. When the results are tabulated for the whole caucus, you will have a fairly accurate idea of how those specific constituents feel about any one kind of issue. This is also good public relations, since voters are flattered to receive that kind of telephone call. "This is Bob Smith's secretary. He wants to know how you feel about tariffs on turnip tops. Would you like a copy of the survey results when they are completed?"

3. AUDIENCE REACTION. Jerry Bruneau, in *The Advance Man*, credits the political success of John Kennedy partly to the fact that he had to obtain the nomination for president through the primary route, which involved hundreds of meetings and intense personal contact with voters. Bruneau says that Kennedy knew an issue was popular because of crowd reactions. Bruneau also explains how Robert Kennedy would change his speeches, depending on the response that he got from his audiences. Both these candidates knew how the public felt. Public meetings, especially those with question periods, would be informative to all candidates. The old-fashioned town meeting, the ultimate public-opinion poll, could yet make a comeback. What is wrong with the Mayor holding a public social occasion once a month in which he answers questions from citizens? It sounds like good television material. You could win an election with a program like that: "Have coffee with the Mayor and tell him what you think." Unfortunately, with the present tendency towards campaigning more and more through the media, people in public life are losing that personal contact with the voters; that loss strengthens the need for effective public-opinion polling.

4. NEWSPAPERS AND MAGAZINES: news, editorials, and letters to the editor. Even the classified ads can

provide information about social and economic trends in a community.

5. SPECIAL-INTEREST GROUPS, such as ratepayers' unions, charities, societies, and fraternal organizations. They will write and tell you how legislative proposals affect them.

6. ELECTIONS IN OTHER JURISDICTIONS, such as municipal in your own or other provinces, or federal. The traditional public-opinion test is the by-election after the death of a sitting member. Governments in power usually lose by-elections, but recover at general elections.

7. QUESTIONNAIRES. A campaign manager should investigate the possibility of combining a public-opinion survey with other activities.
   (a) Enclosed with routine mailings. Ronald Basford, MP, when Minister of Justice, would enclose a questionnaire on current issues along with one of his frequent reports to his constituents. The constituent was invited to complete it and return it to Mr. Basford in Ottawa.
   (b) Handed out at public functions such as non-political meetings, agricultural fairs, or exhibitions.
   (c) Enclosed with the tax bill sent out by municipalities.
   (d) Handed out in point-of-contact locations, such as hamburger chains, lottery-ticket booths, bus stops, and the entrances and exits to public buildings.

8. CANVASSING. All political campaigns involve canvassing, and your canvassers are going to learn a lot on the doorstep. It often happens that canvassers will hear from many householders about the dominance of this issue or that in the minds of voters; yet such facts are seldom drawn to the attention of the party policy-makers. Make sure that all such

valuable information is promptly passed on to the candidate.

John M. Fenton, managing editor of the Gallup Poll, describes in his book *In Your Opinion* the methods of his famous organization.

The Gallup Poll employs about 200 reporters to survey the entire United States, and they poll less than one-tenth of 1 percent of the whole adult population. One-tenth of 1 percent in a typical Canadian constituency is about 50 people. Fenton explains how the Gallup Poll interviewer works.

With each regular assignment, the Gallup Poll interviewer receives a map on which is outlined the area to interview in. This is typically a city block or group of blocks, or, in rural areas, a segment of a township or county. Also indicated on the map are two "starting points". These starting points instruct the interviewer on where he commences two phases of his assignment—one in which he interviews only women, the other, only men.

At about three o'clock in the afternoon on weekdays or at any hour on weekends, the Gallup Poll interviewer proceeds to his first starting point. From there until six he interviews only women. From six o'clock on, interviews are conducted from the second starting point and are made only with men. The division is made in order that men and women will be interviewed at hours when they are normally at home.

At each household in the first half of his assignment, the Gallup Poll interviewer asks to question the youngest woman who is at home who is twenty-one years of age or older.

This age selection plan is based on the known fact that the younger you are, the more chance there is that you will not be at home. By interviewing the young whenever they are encountered, an age distribution is obtained which closely parallels that recorded by the Census Bureau.

If your organization has sufficient money, you

should give serious consideration to obtaining a professional public-opinion organization to conduct carefully selected polling surveys in your constituency; alternatively, you should retain a professional to instruct your volunteer staff.

VOLUNTEER
SURVEYS

Anybody can take a survey. All you need to do is ask a number of people the same question, keep a careful record of their answers, and total up the results. How reliable such a survey would be is another question.

Politicians in Canada do not quite trust political surveys. They are not convinced of their usefulness, probably because they lack knowledge of the technical requirements, and they are concerned about their cost. But, with volunteer help, costs can be kept down considerably.

Each major political party should have a political-survey section in operation at all times. It seems to me that it would be a smart thing for the youth section of a party to establish a permanent polling-survey corporation to assist the adult party in testing the political winds. The youth section could do outside commercial work from time to time in order to earn money for their own affairs, to test their polling procedures, and to continually polish their objectivity.

Polling techniques are not that complicated. Any library will produce a good book on polling techniques. College students can be instructed in about two sessions on how to carry out the interviews necessary to sample opinion in a particular constituency.

RESULTS
ATTAINABLE

Robert Ludwig, a friend of mine, was with the British Army government teams which followed the Allied armies' march across Europe in the Second World War. Mr. Ludwig and his military colleagues would enter German towns as the Allied armies advanced, and would try to get the civic institutions operating again. The first task would be to get the domestic fresh-water system working. Then they would fix the sewers and restore electric power. When the town had settled down, it was Mr. Ludwig's job to get some idea of what the local populace was thinking, for the purpose of aiding government. Mr. Ludwig assembled on paper about 12 groups of 10 people. Each group of 10 was regarded as a separate sample, and he tried to balance each sample by including some rich and some poor, some young and some old, and some men and some women. He found that he could poll the same people several times and get what he believed were accurate results. If all his groups of 10 agreed approximately, one with another, he could assume that he was getting a good cross-sample. If 1 of the groups of 10 was badly out of agreement with the other samples, he made inquiries to discover the reason, or he dropped the group as being unrepresentative of the community.

A candidate or member wants to know how he is doing with the electorate, and if he is not doing well, he will want to know why. In Chapter 4 I gave the example of Nelson Rockefeller, who, as a result of a survey taken eighteen months before the election, found himself in a losing position. He took steps to correct this, and succeeded. Without a perceptive political survey he would not have known about the problem.

The Gallup Poll claims to have guessed the last eight U.S. presidential elections within 3 percent. This degree of accuracy would not suffice everywhere: in many elections, 3-percent swings elect or defeat candidates. Nevertheless, polls do show trends; they can indicate whether you are catching up on the opposition, or vice versa.

Municipal governments should expend tax moneys on surveys, so long as they make the result public. It is good politics, and good government, to ask citizens what they think of garbage collection, police practices, or services from city hall; there is no reason why a city council need be in the dark about such things.

For example, a city police force could check at least twice a year how ordinary citizens feel about their organization, by asking the following questions:

1. How often do you speak to a policeman?

2. The last time you did so, was the policeman pleasant, noncommittal, or rude?

3. Do you feel safe on the streets during daylight hours?

4. Do you feel safe on the streets after dark?

5. When you last required police help, was the help superior, adequate, not adequate, or not obtainable?

6. Why do you think crimes are sometimes not reported?

    (a) People are afraid.

    (b) People do not trust the police.

    (c) People don't think crime is important.

    (d) I do not know.

One municipal survey tested the reaction to a proposed new system of garbage collection in which two families' garbage would be grouped together in one container, so that mechanical devices could be used on the garbage truck. It turned out that most people wanted their garbage to go in four-family rather than two-family groups, so that their own garbage might be less easily identifiable. As you see, you can't think of everything.

I recall a small public-opinion poll being taken within the membership of a political constituency organization to assess the support for a certain candidate at the nominating convention. The idea was to find out who supported whom, and to get that candidate's supporters to the nominating convention without encouraging the others.

DETECT THE TRENDS No modern campaigner can afford to be ignorant of polling techniques. The most important results that you can get from public-opinion surveys are the changes or trends in public attitudes as the campaign proceeds. Such trends are more significant than the result of any one survey. So take surveys regularly over a period of time. Then, even if your polling sample is slightly skewed, you will still be able to spot the trend. If the survey results show you are only holding steady, you will have to work harder or at least become more visible.

WHAT TO ASK   Information which a candidate can put to good use would be:
1. What do your constituents consider the important issues in the coming campaign?
2. What views do those constituents have about the top 5 issues they have selected?
3. What do your constituents think of your opponents?
4. What do the constituents think of your own candidate?
5. What do your constituents like about your program?
6. What do your constituents dislike about your program?
7. What parts of your program do all your constituents approve of?
8. If the person being interviewed were to vote tomorrow, who would he vote for, and why?

ERRORS   It must be pointed out that even elaborate surveys sometimes produce erroneous results. The *Literary Digest* in 1936 polled 2,375,000 people and forecast that Republican nominee Alfred Landon would defeat Franklin Delano Roosevelt in Roosevelt's second run for the presidency. They had sampled automobile owners and telephone subscribers, and, in 1936, those did not represent the average American. A simple, obvious error.

It was the Gallup Poll which erred in forecasting Thomas E. Dewey's victory over Harry Truman in the 1948 presidential election. John Fenton explains the error:

The chief error lay in the fact that practically all of the public opinion polls stopped their interviewing too early in the campaign. With the Gallup Poll, interviewing in the final survey was completed on October 15, eighteen days before Election Day. The survey did not catch the last-minute trend to the Democrats among such groups as Midwestern Farmers, disillusioned Wallace supporters, and wavering voters who made up their minds after hearing one of Truman's "give-'em-hell" speeches in the closing days of the campaign. A post-election analysis showed that a minimum of 4.5 million votes, nearly one out of five in Truman's total vote, were based on decisions by voters after the middle of October.*

CAUSES OF ERROR   Political surveys, as commonly used, are far from infallible. Here are some sources of error.

1. Selecting the sample to be polled: do the 100 or 200 people whom you question accurately represent the whole constituency?

2. Are you using the right kind of interviewers? In the United States they have noticed that black interviewers and white interviewers sometimes get different results when interviewing the same groups of black or white Americans.

3. Are you asking loaded questions? Loaded questions may subtly invite certain answers. Other questions, on delicate subjects, may lead to deliberate lying. For example, if you ask a citizen when was the last time he broke the law, he may not tell the truth. Kenneth Webb and Harry P. Hatry, in *Obtaining Citizen Feedback*,† give a good example of a clumsy questionnaire. In 1971, some blacks were asked in a survey whether they would like to live in a black community or in a predominantly white suburb, if there were no financial or social obstacles to moving. Sixty-eight percent said they preferred to live in a black community. Later, the questionnaire was seen to be inadequate; it was amended to include the third choice of an integrated community. After that change, only 30 percent of the blacks polled opted for living in a black community. The above-mentioned book contains much sound advice on the use of political surveys in municipal affairs.

* John M. Fenton, *In Your Opinion* (Boston: Little, Brown and Company, 1960).

† (Washington, D.C.: The Urban Institute, 1973.)

4. Are your interviewers adequately trained to put the questions correctly and record the answers accurately?

5. Are your constituents adequately informed? If they do not have enough information to decide one way or another on an issue, there is no point in polling them; but if the issue is relevant, it is then your responsibility to try and inform them. A political candidate is something like a teacher and, if he succeeds in reaching his electorate, he can teach them.

6. Are the constituents' real views on a subject masked by some recent event or current condition? For example, do not survey opinion on capital punishment immediately after a brutal murder has taken place in your community. Another example: some Canadians have said that much of the separatists' support in Quebec springs from the high unemployment rate and that, as the Québécois become more prosperous and economically secure, the percentage polled as being in favour of separatism will decline.

7. Do you have adequate information about your own community? For example, when planning a telephone survey, you would naturally refer to the telephone directory. But suppose that 25 percent of the telephones in your town are unlisted, or that 15 percent of the people do not have access to a telephone; those are things you should know before launching a telephone survey.

A POST-ELECTION POLL One week after the 1970 Vancouver civic election, Messrs. Julian Minghi, Harry Swaye, and Dennis Rumley, of the Department of Geography of the University of British Columbia, mailed 2,264 questionnaires to voters in eight typical civic polls. Four of the eight polls were chosen before the election from the economically and socially distinctive areas of the city, and the remaining four polls were chosen on the basis of the results as follows:

1. The poll which most accurately reflected the total mayoralty vote.

2. The poll which most inaccurately reflected the total mayoralty vote.

3. The poll which most accurately reflected the total aldermanic vote.

4. The poll which most inaccurately reflected the total aldermanic vote.

Questionnaires were sent to one voter in six from those eight polls. The names and addresses were obtained from the registered voters' list.

The results analysed what the voters felt were the important election issues. The subjects which most interested the voters were pollution, rapid transit, and law and order. The issues which least interested the voters were the ward system and tenants' rights.

The poll also indicated that one-half of Mr. Campbell's supporters were over fifty-five, that one-half of Dr. Gibson's supporters were under thirty-four, and that Mr. Gargrave's supporters were scattered evenly over the age groups, except that he had no support whatsoever from people sixty-five and older.

It would have been a great help if those three Vancouver mayoralty contestants had possessed that knowledge before the election, when they were preparing their campaign plans and literature.

INTERPRETING
RESULTS

Election candidates, and elected representatives as well, whether in government or in opposition, should remember that a political survey is no substitute for political judgment. You cannot solve problems solely by surveys. Mature minds have to assess the survey results, review the questions, and make decisions based upon facts.

To be sure in some areas feelings are facts. If a black citizen feels that an institution is discriminating against him, the effect on him is just the same whether that institution is or is not actually discriminating. It is important that people in a city feel safe, as well as being safe; perhaps it is more important, because successful social interaction is based upon trust. If some voters feel that a government is incompetent, it makes no difference whether the government is incompetent or not, because those votes will go elsewhere at election-time.

But in other areas, public opinions are not enough; you also have to consider the government's other responsibilities and its available resources. Governments at all levels are deluged with good ideas. The problem is to decide which good idea should receive attention first, or at all, depending upon the availability of resources, which usually means money. I wish all the sidewalks in the city of Vancouver were always in good repair; but sidewalks, like sewers, have to line up for the available money. Elected officials resolve problems after study and research, and then they ask the elector whether he will accept the solution and pay for it.

GETTING ORGANIZED

The following is a checklist which you may find useful if you wish to conduct a survey in your locality.*

1. What information is your candidate seeking?
2. Is the information available elsewhere?
3. How much money is available to spend on this survey?
4. Is the survey to be conducted by personal interview, mail, or telephone?
5. Compose a questionnaire which will get the required information.
6. Select a polling sample which will give you a balanced result.
7. List and train your volunteer pollsters.
8. Test your sample and test your questionnaire.
9. Evaluate your sample and your questionnaire.
10. Take your survey.
11. Review and evaluate your survey results.
12. Make political decisions based upon the survey's results, and accept responsibility for those decisions.

* Webb and Hatry, *Obtaining Citizen Feedback*, p. 44.

Getting Out the Vote

A POLL ORGANIZATION AND THE VOLUNTEER CANVASS
CAN INCREASE YOUR VOTE 10%.

One of the key personnel in a political campaign is the canvass-committee chairman, or poll organizer. In a Canadian federal election, every constituency is divided into polls, each containing approximately 300 voters living in the same area. In the city, a poll may be only one block of apartments. This poll is a manageable microcosm; it is upon this unit that the canvassing system is based.

Canvassing is by far the most important part of the campaign. Everything else is secondary; nothing else should take precedence.

Efficiently conducted, canvassing locates your support. The canvasser who knows his poll, and the people in it, should be able to forecast the result in that poll within 10 votes.

Canvassing brings your campaign into the voter's home. It lets the candidate meet, through his personal representative the poll canvasser, a member of every household in the riding. It gives the voter a chance to consider your program. If the canvasser can develop a two-way rapport with the voters, he can get them to comment on your program, and on other current issues. This feedback from voters should be promptly passed on to campaign headquarters, where it will be a guide for confirming, or, if need be, for modifying, campaign strategy.

Canvassing provides the opportunity for handing literature directly to voters, rather than sending it through the mail. At today's postage rates, this is quite a saving. If no one in the household is at home, you leave your literature; if it is properly drafted, it invites support from the householder and, if anyone wants to help, it tells him what to do.

With good canvassing, you can persuade people to put up posters and signs on their property; you can raise money for campaign funds; and you can get out the vote. You must make sure that every person who says he will vote for your candidate actually does vote on polling day. If you can do this you can increase your vote by 10 percent.

Canvassing is a wonderful way to use intelligent volunteers, and a supporter can get a lot of satisfaction out of canvassing—out of getting to know and understand his own poll. Given a good candidate and an effective political campaign, the poll organization is an unbeatable election technique. The voter should welcome his neighbourhood canvasser, who is helping to make the democratic system work.

FINDING CANVASSERS   The chairman's aim should be to appoint 2 canvassers for every poll in the constituency. Having 2 canvassers per poll improves morale; it gives you a reserve canvasser for each poll; and on election day they can co-operate at their own polling station. One serves inside as a scrutineer, carefully recording each voter as he comes to cast his vote. A runner calls every hour, obtains the numbers of those people who have voted, and takes them to the outside scrutineer, who then consults his canvassing list and makes sure that all known supporters get to the poll by closing time. Simple. But it elects and defeats governments.

The best method of finding canvassers is to keep your poll organization intact between elections by appointing zone captains, each of whom supervises 12 polls and keeps his finger on the pulse of his neighbourhood. A candidate should write a personal note each year to those zone captains.

The system I am recommending is run entirely by volunteer help. The canvass-committee chairman and the zone captains keep records of people who have canvassed before, and they are constantly on the lookout for people who may be suitable as canvassers in the future.

Finding canvassers is not an easy job, but here are some potential sources of recruits.

1. Party membership lists.
2. Supporters' lists.
3. Records of workers in past elections.
4. People who posted signs on their property in past elections.
5. Relatives, friends, and neighbours of candidate and key campaign workers.
6. Potential canvassers found during door-to-door canvassing.
7. Volunteers at public meetings or visitors to the committee rooms.

Remember that for canvassing, carefully instructed, fresh-scrubbed teenagers can do a superb job.

ORGANIZING THE CANVASS   The typical federal constituency has about 160 polls, each poll with about 300 registered voters. You will have prepared a large poll map of your constituency, you will have obtained the results of the last 2 elections, and you will have coloured your poll map to indicate promising areas, winning areas, and losing areas. If you have plenty of help and plenty of time, you will canvass every poll, covering the best polls first. Otherwise, you concentrate your canvassing on the promising and winning areas and ignore the losing areas. Here is a useful overall canvassing plan.

PRE-ELECTION CANVASS.   Canvass every household and check to see if all eligible voters are registered.

FIRST CAMPAIGN CANVASS.   Canvass everyone and try to ascertain voters' intentions. Ask the strong supporters to accept lawn or window signs.

SECOND CAMPAIGN CANVASS.   Skip the "hostiles"; canvass supporters, possibles, and undecideds. Make another push for sign locations.

THIRD CAMPAIGN CANVASS.   As before, skip the "hostiles"; quickly canvass the supporters. Spend more time with possibles and undecideds. Try again for sign locations.

At the earliest opportunity obtain a preliminary voters' list. Each candidate is entitled to 20 copies of this list under Section 18(12) of the *Canada Elections Act*.

The canvass-committee chairman then assigns his canvassers to their polls. It is best, where possible, to assign each canvasser to the poll in which he lives. Most successful canvassers will canvass 3 times during the campaign; the canvassing teams will get to know their polls very well indeed, and will be in a position to squeeze every possible vote out of them on election day.

If you are short of canvassers, assign 2 people to 2 polls; they can act as a team. Another general principle to bear in mind where possible is to assign the best canvassers to the best polls.

Prepare canvassers' kits, each one to contain:

1. A sketch map of that canvasser's poll.
2. A poll book in which will be entered, from the voters' list, all the registered voters in the poll, including their names, addresses, telephone numbers, and occupations, plus all other information gained during the canvassing.
3. A selection of campaign literature.
4. A receipt book for acknowledging donations.
5. Forms which can be filled in by people who want to help with the campaign.

6. Brief written instructions as to canvassing procedure.
7. A timetable showing when to start and when to finish each stage of the canvass.

INSTRUCTING CANVASSERS

The poll organizer should hold 1 or 2 meetings, say 1 in the daytime and 1 in the evening, to issue campaign kits, to keep morale and enthusiasm high, to explain the purpose of the whole operation, to show what will be done with the information when it is gathered, and to give the new recruits some training in what to do on the doorstep. The candidate should be present at these meetings, to add his weight to this extremely valuable process. It is important that every canvasser should know the candidate personally, and it is the candidate's responsibility to know the canvassers; the candidate must make himself available.

The canvassers are told that over a period of several evenings they should call on the 100 or so households in each of their polls, and try to obtain from each household the following information:

1. The names of all voters in the household. Differentiate between the various people in the house.
2. Will the voters at that address be voting?
3. Will they need a car to take them to the poll? If so, when?
4. Will they need a babysitter?
5. If they will not be voting, why not? This question is asked to help prevent impersonation at the polls. For example, if a voter says he will be out of the province on polling day, you will make sure that no impostor votes in his place.
6. How do they intend to vote (if this can be found out diplomatically)?

All this information will be carefully recorded in the canvasser's own poll book, using the symbols mentioned in Chapter 5: S = supporter; P = possible supporter; H = hostile; U = undecided; O = out, not at home.

In these meetings the canvassers are shown, through role-playing, how the work is done; these skits can be hilarious. Do a lot of the role-playing. Don't try to obtain the desired information by asking a series of blunt questions. With the voters' list in hand, and especially with pre-existing knowledge of the area, it should be possible to know and to use the name of the person who answers the door. Open with some indirect remark like this: "Hello, there, Mrs. Voter. I'm your neighbour from across the street; my name is May Smith, and I represent Gordon Fairweather, the Conservative candidate in Fundy-Royal riding. How do you think the election is going to go?" (or substitute a similar lead-in question for the last sentence).

The canvasser is trying to create a favourable impression for the candidate and his program. She is an ambassador, and should look and act like an ambassador.

Often, after such an opening, the voter will tell you who she supports. Even if she does not, it is usually not too difficult to make an accurate guess as to how she will vote. Remember, you cannot take for granted that a husband and wife will vote the same way.

If the voter seems hostile, the canvasser should not get into an argument, but should politely withdraw. If the voter shows interest, the canvasser has literature at hand, ready to give out, and should also be able to talk intelligently about party policy.

Here, in brief, are some useful hints for canvassers:
1. Be neat in dress.
2. Do not ask the permission of apartment managers to canvass their buildings; they may bar your entrance.
3. Do not accept a voter's invitation to enter the residence.
4. Address the voter by name.
5. Always say which candidate you represent.
6. Do not directly ask the voter how he is going to vote.

7. Always be polite; do not get into arguments.
8. Know your party's policy.
9. Know your local committee-room telephone number.
10. Whether the front-door interview is hostile or friendly, keep it brief.

The two members of each team should arrange to meet frequently during each spell of canvassing to exchange information. A novice who has had two doors shut in his face on his first canvass is liable to get a bad case of canvassing blues. It is nice to have a partner as a sort of security blanket.

Much of the value of the canvassing will be lost if each canvasser does not regularly keep the campaign committee informed of opinions and attitudes in his poll. So when the canvasser has finished his morning, or afternoon, or evening canvass, he *must* return to the committee room and report to the poll organizer or his deputy. This reporting lets the organizer know exactly how the canvass is going, and who is and who is not meeting his timetable; it allows prompt action to be taken on the offers of sign space or volunteer help, or on the requests for transportation that the canvassers have received. Moreover, the regular reporting helps to keep up the morale of the canvassing team. If some beginners have difficulties, they can get advice and encouragement from the old hands.

The organizer should regularly check that canvassers' poll-book entries are clear and complete. This is necessary because some emergency may force you to change canvassers in a poll, and the new canvasser must be able to understand his predecessor's records. Moreover, these poll books should all be saved as valuable material for post-election analysis and for planning the next election campaign.

When the canvassing is over and the astute, hard-working, exhausted canvass-committee chairman has done his best to identify and locate his candidate's supporters, then he must arrange to get them to the polling booth with sufficient information to cast a favourable ballot. The mechanics of performing this task will be described in Chapter 13, called "Election Day".

THE KENNEDY
AND McCARTHY
SYSTEMS

Ben Stavis, author of *We Were the Campaign*, has written a whole book on canvassing. It tells the story of Senator Eugene McCarthy's attempt to win the Democratic nomination for President in the U.S. 1968 campaign which culminated in Robert Kennedy's assassination, President Johnson's "resignation", and Hubert Humphrey's nomination for President at the riotous Chicago Cow Palace convention. Mr. Stavis takes you down to the finishing wire, doorknock by doorknock.

Stavis relates how the Robert Kennedy primary campaign used a short-cut canvassing technique. The Kennedy campaigners just phoned at random into a poll until they found supporters. They then mailed those supporters a package of literature and asked them to distribute it to their neighbours. Stavis was describing primary elections in which, I suppose, the party machinery was not available to Kennedy and McCarthy.

Especially fascinating is Stavis's description of what is now called Eugene McCarthy's "children's crusade". During the summer of 1968, unpaid volunteer college students were bussed and flown for hundreds and thousands of miles back and forth across the United States of America, carrying out the various canvassing procedures described in this chapter. Any candidate who could meld the energy and idealism of Canada's university and college students with this kind of poll organization would create a political juggernaut.

DISTRIBUTING
LITERATURE

Another function for your canvassing organization can be the simple distribution of leaflets, without face-to-face contact with the voters. This cannot really be called canvassing, but the canvassers can very well do it. This is a good money-saver; the cost of assembling and delivering *each* leaflet through addressed first-class mail would be about 31 cents. Here are some instructions for this operation.

1. Keep inside the boundaries shown on your poll map. Do only the insides of the streets which form the boundaries; the other sides of those streets are in other polls, and will be covered by different deliveries.

2. Place the leaflet under the front door or through the letter box; do not leave it outside the door. There is no need to knock or ring at the door.

3. On completion of the delivery, return to the committee room the poll map and the undistributed leaflets. Report to the poll organizer that the assigned poll has been covered.

RISKS IN CANVASSING

I think that the canvassing program I have described should be enough for the average constituency. It is quite possible to over-canvass. You can antagonize potential supporters by using improperly instructed canvassers, or by calling too often. By calling too often on opponents you may arouse them to get out and vote, thus producing results opposite to those you intended.

THE BANDWAGON ATMOSPHERE

One important result of well-planned, well-executed canvassing is the stimulating effect it has on your own workers. For some time before an election is called, the party organizers may be reserving rented aircraft for cross-country tours by the leader or starting to lease billboard space. The rank-and-file worker has nothing to do with all that. Yet when you start recruiting canvassers, instructing them and assigning them to their polls, it stirs up a bandwagon atmosphere that begins to create the smell of victory.

GENERAL CANVASS-PLANNING CHECKLIST

Zone captains required:

Zone 1 _____ (Name, address, telephone)
Zone 2 _____ (Name, address, telephone)
etc.

Canvasser recruitment to start _____ to be completed _____

Preliminary voters' list will be available _____ (date)
Canvasser's kit contents:
  Poll maps: No. required _____ Obtained _____
  Written instructions: No. required _____ Obtained

  Poll books: No. required _____ Obtained _____
  Leaflet no. 1: No. required _____ Obtained _____
  Receipt books: No. required _____ Obtained

  Volunteer forms: No. required _____ Obtained

  Timetables: No. required _____ Obtained _____

CANVASSER   1st Session:
INSTRUCTOR'S   Person in charge _____ Date _____ Place _____
CHECKLIST   Time _____
2nd Session:
Person in charge _____ Date _____ Place _____
Time _____
(and so on—as many entries as are needed)

CANVASS-   Pre-election canvass: date to begin _____
SCHEDULE   finish _____
CHECKLIST   1st campaign canvass: date to begin _____
finish _____
2nd campaign canvass: date to begin _____
finish _____
3rd campaign canvass: date to begin _____
finish _____
Literature distribution(s): date(s) _____ finish _____

ZONE   Poll No. _____ Canvassers _____ (Name, address,
CAPTAIN'S   telephone)
CHECKLIST   (and so on—as many entries as are needed)
Canvassers' arrangements to report progress to zone
captain:
Date _____ Time _____ Place _____
(and so on—as many entries as are needed)

Raising Money

DO NOT BE SHY ABOUT ASKING THE PUBLIC
TO FINANCE AN ELECTION CAMPAIGN.

Political parties raise money in different ways.
Although until recently the subject was shrouded in
mystery, it seems to me that political fund-raising
warrants at least a one-semester course at the
university level. *If* participants could be persuaded to
talk, fund-raising could provide enough material for a
dozen doctoral theses.

COLLECTING AT THE TOP — Some parties collect money from their senior echelons
in order to finance a national or provincial umbrella-
campaign across all the constituencies. In this way the
national party ensures a minimum standard of daily
and weekly newspaper advertising and the production
of a common leaflet. The national leader's travel
expenses would also be paid from that national fund.
Small amounts of money might also be sent out by
cheque from the national pool to individual
candidates. A candidate might be granted $200 in cash
plus benefits.
     It is my guess, based on experience, that nearly all
national institutions, such as banks, national
corporations, trade unions, railways, or public utilities
in private hands, contribute money to the political
parties of their choice. It would be a courageous
corporation that would not contribute when the
bagman called. But such an institution can hedge its
bets by contributing to more than one party. I should

think that the national banks and the public utilities give 60 percent to the government and 40 percent to the official opposition in any particular national election.

Since the Watergate scandals and the book *All the President's Men* we know how the Republican party of the United States raises its funds. The Democratic party of the United States, and individual candidates, have gone on national television for the express purpose of raising money. They urge ordinary citizens to contribute in order to release the American national parties from the pressure of large donors. Some big American donors have, in effect, purchased ambassadorships to foreign lands. In England the odd title has been purchased with campaign contributions. *Political Party Financing in Canada* tells the Canadian story, which is no better.

COLLECTING AT THE BOTTOM   Other political parties gather money primarily at the bottom of the organizational pyramid, and from that level it rises to the top. For instance, in 1972 the NDP provincial riding of Vancouver Centre was assigned a quota of $2,800. That meant that before Vancouver Centre could spend any money within the constituency it was required to forward $2,800 to the provincial office to help finance the umbrella campaign over all the constituencies.

The total NDP provincial-office budget at that time would have been about $100,000. In my experience, in British Columbia, the provincial office would actually receive about two-thirds of each provincial quota from the constituencies.

The provincial office also sells posters and leaflets at cost to the constituencies. Since this printing can be done in huge quantities, it is to the constituencies' benefit to purchase a basic leaflet and a basic poster. Naturally the leadership wants a degree of uniformity in style and colour across the whole province, to help create that bandwagon effect that every campaign manager strives for.

The provincial office also receives contributions directly from donors. Many of these supporters do not belong to any specific party organization.

To sum up, then, the provincial funding consists of: (a) money from constituency quotas; (b) receipts from sale of campaign literature; (c) contributions directly to the provincial office. Most of this provincial budget is spent on the overall provincial campaign. On rare occasions the NDP provincial office makes small contributions to individual candidates in isolated areas.

ASKING FOR IT   Thus you have the two systems: on the one hand, gathering money at the top, running an umbrella campaign, and letting some money filter down to the constituencies; on the other hand, money raised at the bottom comes in to headquarters to finance the broad campaign built around the party leader. Some political parties use combinations of both systems. But the common characteristic of all the financial systems I am familiar with is that, for constituency campaign expenses, the local candidate is on his own, with minimal assistance from the central office. The candidate and his campaign committee have to scratch for their own funds, and that is what this chapter is about.

It sounds simple, and it is simple. The only way to get money for an election campaign is to ask for it.

COLLECTING   I must emphasize what I said in Chapter 1: the task of
AND SPENDING   collecting money should be kept separate from the business of spending it. Raising funds is a full-time job for the finance chairman; whoever holds that position should have no other function, and he should be one of your best people.

The treasurer's duty is to keep track of all expenditures, to see that nobody spends a dollar without written authorization, and to see that he gets a receipt for every dollar disbursed. Anybody who spends campaign funds without written authority should foot the bill himself. Be strict about this, and pounce on the first violator.

STRIKING A   As the first stage in any realistic financial campaign,
BUDGET   the campaign committee meet and strike a budget.
They should approach the problem from two angles.
First they decide what they would *like* to do in terms
of waging a campaign; secondly, they consider how
much money they can raise. If it is a federal
campaign, they look at the *Canada Elections Act* and
calculate the maximum amount that the *Act* would
permit them to spend. They should deduct 10 percent
from the maximum, then build the budget upon the
resulting sum of money. I suggest deducting that 10
percent for emergencies, because you must not spend
more than the maximum prescribed by statute, and
you do not want to cripple your campaign by being
prohibited from spending small amounts of money on
last-minute emergencies.

Note that the legal restrictions on federal election
spending refer to the 58 days between issuance of the
writ and election day, so campaign funds spent *before*
issuance of the election writ are exempt from these
provisions.

Current Canadian income-tax law allows deduction
of a percentage of all contributions to registered
political parties or candidates. The deduction is taken,
not from the donor's taxable income, but from his
federal tax payable. In other words, you can divert
federal tax revenue directly to your political party.
The following table gives a few examples of income-
tax credits that can be claimed.

Total contributions during the year	Calculation	Tax Credit
$10	(75% of $10)	$7.50
$50	(75% of $50)	$37.50
$100	(75% of $100)	$75.00
$550	($75 + 50% of $450)	$300.00
$850	($300 + 33⅓% of $300)	$400.00
$1150	($300 + 33⅓% of $600)	(Maximum) $500.00
$1400	(Maximum $500)	$500.00

Your finance committee must be familiar with the procedure in order to advise contributors.

If you have no prior budgeting experience to draw upon, you should ask yourself how much money you can raise, and that should give you an approximate total for your budget. There is a checklist at the end of this chapter that will give you considerable help in putting the budget together. This list is divided into two parts: how much you can raise, and how much you will need. You hope that both parts will balance.

Here are three sample budgets (based on 1976 expenses) that will illustrate some of the customary features.

LOW-LEVEL BUDGET FOR A CIVIC ELECTION

Summary (estimates)

Committee rooms	$1,200.00
Literature	2,800.00
Signs	700.00
Meetings	60.00
Publicity	900.00
Salaries	0.00
Miscellaneous	250.00
Total	$5,910.00

Details

Committee Rooms	Rents	$ 375.00
	Phones	175.00
	Lights	50.00
	Supplies	200.00
	Stamps	400.00
		$1,200.00
Literature	Introductory leaflet	$1,000.00
	2nd leaflet	400.00
	Poll card	1,000.00
	Letterheads	100.00
	Candidate's literature	100.00
	Special literature	200.00
		$2,800.00

Signs	4' x 8's	$ 450.00
	Window cards	250.00
		$ 700.00
Meetings	Supplies	$ 60.00
Publicity	Daily papers	$ 400.00
	Weekly and ethnic papers	300.00
	Dinner	200.00
		$ 900.00
Miscellaneous		$ 250.00
	Total	$5,910.00

BUDGET FOR A RURAL CONSTITUENCY IN A
PROVINCIAL ELECTION

Expenditures (estimates)

2 household mailings	$ 800.00
2,000 posters	400.00
Candidate's expenses	250.00
Constituency headquarters rent	200.00
General postage	50.00
Radio	450.00
Weekly newspaper advertisements	400.00
Telephone	100.00
Leaflets	350.00
Public meetings (less collections)	10.00
Miscellaneous	100.00
Plywood for billboards	100.00
Salaries	0.00
Total	$3,210.00

BUDGET FOR AN URBAN CONSTITUENCY IN A FEDERAL ELECTION

Receipts (actual)

Collections at meetings	$ 3,376.10
Individual donations	7,208.40

Special contributions	4,000.00
Donations from institutions	7,768.00
Miscellaneous	11.00
Total receipts	$22,363.50

Disbursements (actual)

Candidate's deposit	$ 200.00
Hall rentals	480.00
Outside speakers' expenses	250.00
Posters	2,784.30
Miscellaneous	1,008.20
Contribution to federal quota	6,007.50
Candidate's personal letter	3,303.80
Advertising	3,121.00
Telephone	571.10
Refund to national office	220.00
Nominating convention	96.00
Bank charges	13.60
Total expenditures	$18,055.50
Transferred to permanent campaign fund	$ 4,308.00
	$22,363.50

A WORD OF
WARNING

It may be necessary, early in the campaign, to amend the budget up or down; this can be done, after careful analysis, discussion, and approval, by the campaign committee. But it is inexcusable to overspend the budget through inadequate accounting control. If that happens, critics within your organization will say that the overexpenditure was not necessary; and political parties or candidates who fail to pay their money debts after an election will be sure to lose face in their communities.

If your candidate wins, but you are left with a serious deficit, the struggle to pay off that deficit may cripple and depress your organization for years. And if your candidate loses, and you are in debt for campaign expenses, unless you have a very strong, well-knit organization, such as a political party, you will never pay it off.

There is no justification for such a failure. It is comparatively easy to raise money during an election campaign. Your supporters are excited and enthusiastic; it is my experience that they will always respond if you tell them in detail why you want the money and how you are going to spend it, and if they see that your goals are realistic.

THE NUTS AND BOLTS   The budget, drawn up with such care, is not to remain the property of the campaign committee; early in the campaign it should be passed on to the members of your organization. One good method of doing this is by calling a special meeting. Obviously, for this meeting to be a success, there must be careful preparation and a lot of organization. If you keep the following points in mind your meeting should be a success.

1. You need copies of the budget, so that your supporters will know just how much money is to be spent, and where it is going. I suggest that the budget be typed on one side of a letter-sized sheet of white bond paper. It can be mimeographed, Xeroxed, or printed by a photo-ready offset printing house. There is a minor problem of security involved: you do not want your opponents to get copies of your budget.

2. You need another leaflet of the same size, describing your political objectives, your candidate, the sort of campaign you intend to conduct, and the opposition that you face. Do not skimp on details here: for example, if the campaign manager believes that he must get leaflets into every home and erect a hundred and fifty 4' x 8' plywood signs on front lawns, he must tell his supporters so, and estimate the cost. If a full-time person must be hired, the campaign manager must explain why. The campaign manager will have something to say in this leaflet about democracy, the common good, and effective regional representation. The candidate will explain the dangers of defeat, and the benefits of victory. Do not stress personal gain or short-term objectives.

When your 2 leaflets are ready, call a meeting of your political supporters, distribute the leaflets, and explain the nuts and bolts of electioneering. Be frank with your supporters; you are asking them to part with money that they might prefer to spend on personal luxuries. You are asking them to make sacrifices, so make it abundantly clear that the candidate and the campaign committee, too, are going to make sacrifices.

After the candidate has spoken, the supporters should be asked to offer pledges. Careful preparations here will get this pledging session off to a flying start. Suppose, for example, that you are trying to raise $20,000, and you can realistically expect to have 100 people at the meeting; that means they must donate, on the average, $200 each. The campaign manager has spoken in advance to 4 or 5 people, and they have agreed to pledge to raise $200 or more each. That means that each of them will go out and ask 10 people for $20 each, or fail to fulfil his pledge.

Others will be asked before the meeting to pledge smaller amounts in cash, as well as to volunteer their time and services to the campaign in various ways. For example, a full-time person on the front-office telephone for 30 days is a pretty valuable contribution.

Another form of prearranged contribution might be to pledge $15 a month for the next 12 months, and give to the chairman of the meeting, in open session, 12 postdated cheques for a total of $180. The individual could then make a donation of $20 in cash at the meeting in order to complete his quota of $200.

The announcement of all these pledges and donations should, if the meeting goes well, create a mood of confident enthusiasm that will lead to the offering of still more pledges; plenty of pledge forms should be at hand. A sample form is given at the end of this chapter.

This meeting is a good time to announce various other money-raising activities that are planned: selling

jazzy campaign buttons, lotteries (where they are
legal), social activities such as dances and dinners,
sales or raffles of articles donated by supporters, and
so on.

A long vertical poster can then be unwound, shaped
like a giant thermometer, graduated from zero at the
bottom up to $20,000 at the top. A collection is taken
by passing the hat and the finance chairman colours
the bottom of the thermometer in red to indicate the
amount of actual cash that has been raised at the
meeting. With that symbolic colouring of the thermometer, the campaign to raise the money will
have been started.

The collection should then go into a special bank-
account with special signing officers, and the contents
of that account should be regarded as trust money.

Very shortly after this meeting there should be a
review of the results. If realistic estimates of other
money-raising activities, plus the cash and pledges
obtained at the meeting, are enough to meet the
budget, all well and good. But if you cannot obtain
enough pledges to complete your budget, there is
something wrong with your organizational structure,
or with your budget.

THE PYRAMID
SYSTEM
Instead of holding a meeting for public pledging, you
can use a method similar to that mentioned at the
beginning of the chapter under "Collecting at the
Top". The pyramid system of raising money is based
upon organization rather than enthusiasm. It is an
eyeball-to-eyeball technique in which potential donors
are approached in their own homes and offices.

This method can work well if it is properly applied,
but it has been my experience that some finance
chairmen spend too much time personally asking
people for money, and not enough time constructing
the pyramid—a group of trained callers to go out and
do the asking. In other words, the pyramid starts and
ends with the finance chairman; but a good finance
chairman is too valuable to be misused. The finance

chairman should gather a group of a dozen or so people around him, and *those* people go out on the financial canvass.

The usual first step is for the campaign manager, the candidate, and the president of the constituency association to draw up a list of potential donors. The first names on the list will be the members of your organization. Some of those members will only be able to give $20; some will agree to raise money from others, or donate services; other members can give, or will promise to raise, larger sums of money. To this list can be added the friends, supporters, and family of the candidate—people who are not members of your organization, yet are among those hundreds who, in the excitement of an election campaign, come forward and want to take part. Do not forget: people want part of the action; they want to contribute. All you have to do is ask.

You should have carefully preserved the donors' list from the last election; and if your organization has conducted itself with propriety and honour since then, those former donors will probably give again— especially if you have kept in touch with them.

So the updated list of donors is compiled, containing names, addresses, telephone numbers, and perhaps occupations. Then the designated member of the committee knocks on the person's door and says, "I am representing Candidate Smith, and we would like to ask you for a campaign donation." People who are asked to contribute should be given a copy of the budget, and it should be explained to them what use will be made of their contributions. It is high time that we did away with all the mystery surrounding the bagman and the financing of elections.

During the same visit, you can ask the listed donor whether he knows anybody else who might like to contribute. All this can be done simply and politely. There does not have to be any offence given or taken, and often friendships are formed as a result of these calls.

It is important that your financial committeemen be told to place full names, and correct addresses and telephone numbers on all receipts they issue. Federal political donors are entitled to special income-tax deductions, so accuracy is important. If someone gives $200 and expects to deduct $125 of it in cash from his income tax payable, he will need the official receipt, and if he does not get it, he is going to be upset. This must be constantly supervised throughout the campaign.

Moreover, those carbon-receipt counterfoils will be valuable raw material for the next election campaign. When you get into the swing of running elections, you will learn to throw nothing away.

I once watched a senator, on television, describe how he raised money for the Liberal party in an Ontario provincial election. From a magazine he got a list of all the industrial firms in the province, and he made up a card for each firm. He and his wife and daughter prepared these cards on their kitchen table. He then divided the cards into sets of ten, and persuaded some of his friends to go around and call on those industrial firms. He said they did not get much from any one firm, but the total amount was a useful addition to their campaign funds. The point is that in order to get money you have to ask for it.

THE TELEPHONE　Another useful method of raising money is for the candidate, the campaign manager, the finance chairman, and the president of your constituency association to get on the telephone and solicit funds. For this technique it might be wise to wait until after the election is actually called, so that a feeling of excitement is in the air, and the urgent need for money provides donors with an immediate motive to give. You can approach individuals who are known to be potential donors, organizations, corporations, and unions.

Each person telephoned should receive by mail copies of those 2 previously mentioned leaflets setting out your budget and political objectives. You can also advise donors that they may contribute in instalments— modest sums monthly, spread over 1 year. It has been found that total contributions are always vastly increased by this method. To those who accept this plan, you should also mail 12 postdated cheques and a stamped, addressed envelope for easy return of the cheques. If the donor is entitled to income-tax diversion for his contribution, that should be carefully explained to him over the telephone and in the follow-up mailed material. Try, "A donation of $100 only costs you $25."

These are the days of credit cards; people can now donate over the telephone by merely giving you a Master Charge or Visa number. Your finance chair-man should have a visit, ahead of time, with your community officers of Visa and Master Charge.

DIRECT MAIL   Voters are now accustomed to receiving mass-produced letters and blank cheques from churches, charities, and entertainment producers. Direct mail can be used for raising campaign funds, although the process is expensive for printing, addressing, and mailing. The key to success with this technique is the use of a responsive mailing list, which should be built up over the years. In a mobile society, mailing lists quickly become obsolete, so constant updating is essential.

Direct mail is also a useful way to reach people who have not yet been involved in political-party activity; such people may wish to volunteer as well as give money. Computers can be used to select suitable names for this kind of "prospecting".

For drafting texts of appeal letters, see the suggestions in Chapter 8.

COMMITTEE   A rather savage way to get the campaign committee
GUARANTEES   and finance committee to work hard is to persuade them all to endorse notes for campaign borrowings. The total loan should be divided into as many promissory notes as there are committee members, so

that each member guarantees his fair share of the budget. This method usually increases their diligence in raising money from other sources. It also produces cash "up front" early in the campaign, when it is sorely needed.

PASSING
THE LIST
One technique used by churches is to assign a list of potential contributors to each member of the finance committee. The committee member writes his own name, address, and contribution at the head of the list and then hands it to the first potential contributor for him to insert his name, address, and amount of contribution. Each donor in turn looks over the list, sees what the other people have given, and so is encouraged to give generously himself.

It is good strategy to approach the big donors first, so as to give maximum stimulus to the others. The committeeman will also feel obliged to show leadership by making a significant contribution.

CAMPAIGN
LITERATURE
I think that most pieces of campaign literature should ask for public support, either in cash or in personal service. This appeal should give every detail that makes things easier for potential donors: a telephone number at which someone will be on duty all day, and a complete postal address for mailed contributions. At this address someone should always be on hand to welcome anyone who drops in to ask questions, give cash, or offer services.

LEGAL
RESTRICTIONS
Many jurisdictions have rules and regulations defining how candidates and their campaign committees may obtain and spend money. I will describe some of them here; but legislation on the subject varies from time to time and from place to place, so be sure to check your relevant statutes before starting to raise money for your campaign.

BUDGET
CEILINGS
The *Canada Elections Act* limits the amount of money that a political party may spend on a federal election to 30 cents per voter. This means that, for a riding of,

say, 35,000 voters, the national party may spend only 35,000 x 30¢ = $10,500.

The same act limits the spending by a local campaign organization to $1 per name for the first 15,000 names on the voters' list, plus 50 cents per name for the next 10,000, plus 25 cents per name for all in excess of 25,000. So in the same 35,000-voter riding, the local budget limit would be $15,000 + $5,000 + $2,500 = $22,500. These limits apply only to spending after the federal election writs are issued.

Your finance chairman and treasurer will need to keep a careful check on receipts and expenditures, because, after the election, political parties and candidates must file returns and issue official receipts. Call on your election officials and get copies of the statutes and any advisory leaflets that are available to help you fulfil the requirements and perform the duties prescribed. Alternatively, copies of the *Canada Elections Act* 1974 and additional clarification on election expenses are available from the Chief Electoral Officer, 440 Coventry Road, Ottawa, Ontario, K1A 0M6.

It should be understood that the above-mentioned limits on expenditures in a federal election apply not only to money, but also to the commercial value of goods and services used in the campaign, *except volunteer labour.*

The above-mentioned totals of cost, goods, and services are relatively low nowadays, so campaign managers will have to be increasingly cautious in assigning priorities to the various items in their budgets. The volunteer worker will become more valuable because his expenditure of effort is not restricted. In the future one can expect to hear campaign managers telling donors, "Thanks for that $100 cheque. Now get that jacket off, and start delivering those leaflets."

The *Canada Elections Act* provides that a candidate must pay election expenses only through his official agent. Then, 60 days after the election, that official agent must file with the Returning Officer a statement of the candidate's total election expenditure. Each political party must also appoint an auditor who is required to report on financial statements made by the party or the candidate; the Receiver General of Canada will pay up to $250 for this auditing.

The party's statement of election expenses will be published in a newspaper circulating in the electoral district. Publication of this information helps to make the democratic structure of Canada independent of large donors. The source of a political party's funds tells you a lot about that party. If political parties obtain their campaign funds from a wide political and financial base, our civil rights become that much more secure. A member of a legislature who has a thousand donors backing him is less subject to pressure than a member who has only two or three donors and is answerable to them, or, perhaps worse, a candidate who has financed his own campaign and feels that he is answerable to no one.

WHO GIVES WHAT?

It is an offence under the *Provincial Elections Act* of British Columbia for a candidate to make donations for any purpose during a campaign, and it is an offence to solicit donations from a candidate. The *Act* thus protects the candidate from a shakedown.

No person may make a political contribution out of funds which do not belong to him.

Federal political parties and candidates are required to disclose the name of any person who makes a contribution in excess of $100.

MEDIA CONTROLS

Section 61.2 of the *Canada Elections Act* prohibits political advertising in periodicals and political broadcasting on radio and television except for the last 4 weeks of the campaign. Then all such advertising is banned again on the Sunday before polling day and on polling day itself. One purpose of the new section is to reduce the costs of advertising to the competing parties.

Section 99.3 ensures that a magazine, newspaper, radio station, or television station may not put up its rates at election time. The media must not charge more than their usual lowest rates to candidates or parties buying advertising space, after the election writ is issued. The media usually want cash in advance.

COMPENSATION FOR EXPENSES

Section 63.1 of the *Canada Elections Act* introduces a new principle—the compensation of candidates for the cost of distributing literature to voters. The candidate, if he got 15 percent of the votes cast, on making his return of election expenses will get a cheque from the Receiver General for the cost of printing his campaign literature, plus the cost of first-class mailing for that literature. Candidates in the far north will also get a $3,000 allowance for travelling expenses. The Canadian Broadcasting Corporation already allows free-time broadcasts.

All of this shows a trend towards equalizing campaign costs and opportunities between candidates.

MONEY-RAISING CHECKLIST

Here is a checklist for money-raising activities, arranged in chronological order.

1. *Before* the election is called:

   (a) Appoint finance chairman with full authority to organize money-raising committee.

   (b) Start far ahead of time to hold money-raising events like dances, socials, and raffles.

   (c) Obtain as much money as possible, in cash or by pledges, before the election writs are issued.

   (d) Carefully estimate what you can raise, using the following receipts checklist.

RECEIPTS

Surplus from the last election   _____
Expected donations:
   _____ @ $200.00 =
   _____ @ $100.00 =
   _____ @ $ 50.00 =
   _____ @ $ 20.00 =
   _____ @ $ 10.00 =
   _____ @ $ 5.00 =

Miscellaneous   = _____
Total donations   _____
Special-name contributions: make list

                         =

                         =

                         =

                         = _____

Total special-name contributions   _____
Raffles   _____
Banquets and socials   _____
Membership fees   _____
Meeting collections   _____
Other   _____
                         Total receipts   _____
Special assistance, e.g. donated services   _____
Bank loan: list about 20 co-signers   _____

(e) Carefully estimate what your expenses will be, using the following checklist

EXPENDITURES

Deposit ($200 for federal election)   _____
Special expenditures before election writ issued   _____
Quota, if any, to federal umbrella-campaign   _____
Committee room:
   Rent   =
   Light   =
   Phone   =
   Supplies   =
   Postage   = _____
   Total: committee room   _____
Printing:
   Calling cards   _____ @ _____ =
   1st leaflet   _____ @ _____ =
   2nd leaflet   _____ @ _____ =
   Final leaflet   _____ @ _____ =
   "Vote at" cards   _____ @ _____ =
   Letterheads   _____ @ _____ =
   Ethnic literature   _____ @ _____ =
   Photos   _____ @ _____ =
   Other   _____ @ _____ = _____
   Total: printing   _____
Advertising:
   Dailies   =
   Weeklies   =

Others	=	
TV, Radio	= _____	
Total: advertising		_____
Signs:		
Sign-shop rent	=	
2' x 3' silk-screen	=	
Other equipment	=	
4' x 8' x ¼" plywood	=	
Lawn signs _____ @ _____	=	
Window signs _____ @ _____	=	
Stakes, nails, etc.	=	
Committee-room sign	=	
Profilm stencil	=	
Paint, white _____ @ _____	=	
black _____ @ _____	=	
blue _____ @ _____	=	
Lapel buttons _____ @ _____	=	
Truck rental	=	
Bumper-stickers _____ @ _____	=	
Other	= _____	
Total: signs		_____
Meetings:		
Working lunches	=	
Public meetings	=	
Coffee parties	=	
Public banquets	=	
Parades	= _____	
Total: meetings		_____
Staff:		
Salaries	=	
Expenses	= _____	
Total: staff		_____
Other:		
Bank charges	=	
Election-day expenses	=	
Special events	=	
Miscellaneous	= _____	
Other: total		_____
Total expenditures		_____
Deficit or surplus	=	_____

2. *After* the election is called:
(a) Campaign committee adopts the budget.

(b) Full constituency executive approves the budget.

(c) Finance chairman confirmed in his post.

(d) Appoint official agent and duplicate special expenditure vouchers he will need.

(e) Obtain bank loan with required number of co-signers.

(f) If receipts are higher or lower than expected, review and amend the budget before the whole campaign committee. Firmly decide that the budget is not to be exceeded.

(g) Collect all donations or immediate pledges before polling day: it will be hard to do it afterwards.

3. *After* polling day:

(a) Be sure all campaign bills are paid.

(b) Official agent publicly reports all expenditures.

SAMPLE PLEDGE FORM

Name of Party

Name of Constituency

FEDERAL ELECTION PLEDGE

I wish to help elect our candidate in the next federal election. To ensure a victory, I wish to donate $_____ on or before _____, 19____, at $_____ per month.

I will also help by:

1. Secretarial work ☐
2. Scrutineering on election day ☐
3. Canvassing by phone ☐
4. Erecting street signs ☐
5. Addressing envelopes ☐
6. Soliciting for funds ☐
7. Displaying signs ☐
8. Distributing literature ☐
9. Canvassing door to door ☐
10. Joining the party ☐
11. Loaning my car or light truck ☐
12. Holding a house party or meeting ☐
13. Driving a car ☐
14. Other (please explain) ☐

I would like a receipts book   □

NAME_____PHONE_____

ADDRESS _____

Please hand this form in or mail to:
Address: Telephone:
Office hours:

SAMPLE LETTER
TO REQUEST
FUNDS *Name of Party*
Name of Constituency
Candidate: Committee Room:
Finance Chairman: Address:
                                        Phone:
Dear Party Member (Supporter; Constituent; Friend?):
The federal election has now been called, and though
preparations for the election are well under way, we will
need to raise funds to elect our candidate, Bill Smith.
    We need $20,000. We already have $1,000 on hand,
which leaves $19,000 to be raised by donations from
members, supporters, and the public. We need this money
for printing literature, putting up street signs, printing
posters, and paying the rent for our committee room. I
enclose with this letter a detailed estimate of our election
budget along with a table showing how your campaign
contributions can be deducted from your income tax
payable when you file your income-tax return. If you
donate $100 to the campaign, you may deduct $75 from
your income tax payable. Yes, that is right, from your
income tax payable!
    A member of the Finance Committee will be calling upon
you within the next two weeks to provide you with a copy
of the first election leaflet straight from the printers and to
explain to you how political contributions may be deducted
from your income tax. We do need cash now but, if you
wish, you may spread your contributions over twelve
months with postdated cheques, and our financial
committeeman will have those cheques on hand. You no

doubt know other people who would like to support our candidate, and if so, please pass on their names.

The election is going to be a difficult one, and we need all the help we can get. By investing in the election you are helping to ensure good government. If you wish, you can bring in your donation to our committee rooms, or telephone us and we will send someone over to pick up the contribution.

Yours gratefully,
SIGNATURE
Finance Chairman

Election Day

IT COMES SOONER THAN YOU THINK.

This is the moment of truth. The federal campaign which started 2 months ago has drawn to a close and tomorrow morning the polls will open. Are you ready?

A political party's election-day machine has 4 main functions:

1. To ensure that the voting is conducted in accordance with the provisions of the relevant elections act.

2. To get all your identified favourable voters to the polling places before 7:00 p.m.

3. To ensure that the ballots are counted promptly and correctly.

4. To transmit the results of the ballot-counting to your own party headquarters.

These functions may sound simple, but they are very important. Good or bad election-day arrangements can win or lose elections. That is more than you can say about some campaigns.

As a rule, election days in Canada go quite smoothly. Some deputy returning officers may get a little uppity towards the end of the day, when most members of polling-station teams are feeling tired and tense; but that is about all. There is no police supervision of the Canadian election machinery; there is no need for it. The election is conducted by your fellow voters, your neighbours. They are all part-time

workers, across the whole of Canada. There is no
bureaucracy.

THE POLLING
STATION

The *Canada Elections Act* puts a returning officer in
charge of each constituency, and prescribes 1 polling
station for each poll. Sometimes, for convenience, the
constituency returning officer will group 6 polling
stations under 1 roof, in a school or other public
building; indeed, he is required to locate his polling
stations in public buildings where possible. Sometimes
1 poll will have its own separate polling station.

Whether separate or grouped, the polling stations
must have an outer door for admitting voters and, if
possible, another door by which the voters may leave
after they have voted. Inside the polling station is a
booth to which the voter may go in order to mark his
ballot privately.

A deputy returning officer is appointed to run
each polling station; he has a poll clerk to assist him.
The physical equipment, all provided by the
constituency returning officer, includes a poll book,
a voters' list containing the names of registered voters,
the ballot box, a supply of ballot slips, and some
writing instruments, preferably black lead pencils. The
ballot slips are printed locally.

THE INSIDE
SCRUTINEER

In addition to the deputy returning officer and the
poll clerk, 1 or 2 agents of each candidate may remain
in the polling station. In this book I have called these
agents scrutineers. *Scrutineer* is a good word, going
back to 1557, and meaning "one who examines votes
or checks the voting procedure". Usually each party
or candidate has 1 scrutineer in each polling station.
Scrutineers may come and go during the day to spell
each other off, so long as each one is properly
authorized by the candidate or his official agent. But
in my opinion it is best for 1 scrutineer to stay all
day. Take the day off work, get there early, and stay
to see the ballots counted; that way it is more fun.
The scrutineer should realize that he is an essential

part of the election machinery, no less important than the deputy returning officer and the poll clerk.

If you are serving as an inside scrutineer, the election-day manager should provide you with a kit containing:

(a) your credentials

(b) your instructions

(c) an unmarked copy of the voters' list for your poll

(d) 2 or more pens or pencils

(e) a small scratchpad

(f) a ruler

(g) a non-partisan poll badge

A scrutineer should get to the polling station at least three-quarters of an hour before the poll opens. He presents his credentials and, if necessary, he can help the deputy returning officer and poll clerk with setting up tables and chairs and with all the routine of getting the polling station ready for the arrival of the first voter.

All inside scrutineers should have comfortable seats and convenient desks or tables for writing, in full view of the voting process. If there is not enough room or furniture at the polling station for scrutineers, an early complaint should be made to the constituency returning officer.

Each scrutineer is required to be sworn in as an agent of the candidate. A scrutineer must not wear any partisan political identification such as a badge, button, or coloured ribbon; and he should see that nobody else in the polling place wears any such political identification.

It is important that the scrutineers, deputy returning officer, and poll clerk work together as a team to get the job done efficiently and with a minimum of friction.

ELECTION One reason for the presence of scrutineers at every
FRAUDS polling station is to help prevent the perpetration of any fraud. So, for the guidance of scrutineers, I will

describe some of the more common types of fraud, and in each case indicate how it may be detected.

1. THE PRE-STUFFED BALLOT BOX. The scrutineer should examine the ballot box and make sure it is empty before it is locked and sealed by the deputy returning officer first thing in the morning. Norris Denman, in his book *How To Organize an Election*, advises that scrutineers should also scratch the bottom of the ballot box, to make sure that it does not have a false paper bottom.

2. FORGED BALLOTS. It is necessary to guard against forged ballots being placed in the box at any stage of the voting process. That is why certain procedures for handing out, marking, and depositing the ballots are prescribed: the initialling of the unmarked ballot slip with its numbered counterfoil, and then the removal of that counterfoil before the marked, folded ballot is put into the box. Alert scrutineers will see that these anti-forgery precautions are faithfully carried out.

3. BRIBED VOTERS. In this fraud, voters are paid to vote a certain way. An ingenious little procedure ensures that the briber gets his money's worth.
   (a) The briber gives the voter a ballot already marked in the desired way; the voter hides it on his person.
   (b) The voter goes to the polling station, gives his name in the usual way, and gets a new ballot slip.
   (c) He enters the polling booth and pretends to mark the ballot slip; but actually he pockets the new one and brings out the pre-marked one.
   (d) He gives that pre-marked ballot slip to the deputy returning officer, sees it deposited in the box, and leaves.
   (e) Outside the polling station, the voter hands the new, unmarked ballot slip to the briber and then gets paid. The whole process is repeated again and again.

Notice that, to get this process started, the briber needs to have only one authentic, unmarked ballot slip stolen from the polling station early in the day. It is done by a registered voter, or someone posing as a registered voter, who turns up, gets his ballot slip in the usual way, and goes into the polling booth. However, he does not vote; he just puts the unmarked ballot slip in his pocket and walks out of the polling station. To check this fraud, scrutineers should be alert to stop voters removing ballot slips from the polling station.

4. IMPERSONATION. Someone who is bent on serious election fraud finds out the names of people who will not be voting, or arranges for the false registration of imaginary or dead voters; then he provides impersonators to vote under those names. It is a fairly simple fraud to execute, and in close contests it can decide the result of an election. Preventive action against this fraud must be taken in 3 stages.

(a) *Accurate enumeration.* To prevent enumeration fraud, the *Canada Elections Act* provides that in urban areas enumerators shall work in pairs, and that the 2 enumerators shall be nominated by the candidates with the highest and second-highest vote-counts in the previous election. The presumption is that the enumerators of different political parties will be watching each other. So, if some of your supporters are thus appointed as enumerators, warn them to take care that the enumeration is accurate; for example, they should be cautious about suggestions that they split up and simultaneously cover opposite sides of a street, or that they work different floors of an apartment block, in order to get the task done faster.

In rural areas where, presumably, people know one another better, the returning officer appoints the enumerators, 1 only to each poll.

(b) *Thorough canvassing.* I will mention again that one of the duties of the canvasser is to find out who is *not* going to vote on election day in any particular poll. Some registered voters might have died or moved away; some might be nonexistent, the results of crooked enumeration; some genuine, live voters may simply not be interested. The good canvasser notes all this in his records, and the information is eventually passed to the inside scrutineer for that poll.

(c) *Checking at the poll.* The scrutineer, provided with this list of non-voters, will be on the lookout all day for anyone trying to vote under any of those names, will challenge such a person via the deputy returning officer, and will see that the suspect provides thorough proof of identity.

Unfortunately, many of these impersonation frauds are never discovered. Many years ago, Angus MacInnis told me an apocryphal story about Mackenzie King. One day, Prime Minister King was visiting in an Ontario town and inquired as to the whereabouts of an old political enemy. Told that his opponent had passed on, Mr. King asked to visit the grave. A local supporter took him to the cemetery. As he read the headstone, Mackenzie King removed his hat and said, "This man fought hard against me at many an election." The local supporter, so goes the tale, replied, "Mr. King, he has voted for you many times since his death."

WHO MAY VOTE? To be prepared for any disputes or challenges as to who can and who cannot vote, scrutineers should know something of how the voters' list is compiled.

Every man and woman who has attained the age of 18 years on or before the polling day, and is a Canadian citizen, is entitled to vote, if he is on the voters' list.

Every citizen should make it his business to get on the voters' list. After the election is called, preliminary lists of voters are mailed to each urban household, or posted in each locality. If a resident is qualified, but finds that his name is not on the preliminary list, he should then read the instructions on the list and take steps to place himself on it by going to the Court of Revision.

In urban areas a person whose name is not on the final voting list may not vote. In rural areas a person who has been inadvertently left off the voters' list may vote by taking a special oath at the poll.

THE VOTING PROCEDURE The voter enters by the front door and goes to the table at which are seated the deputy returning officer and the poll clerk. He gives his name, and the poll clerk crosses that name off the voters' list so that that person may not vote again.

At the same time the clerk announces the voter's name and number aloud. The scrutineer draws a line through that name on his own copy of the list and writes the voter's number on his scratchpad. Some election-day managers give their scrutineers printed poll-slips; these are simply pieces of paper with numbers from 1 to 350 printed on them. Then, instead of writing the voter's number, the inside scrutineer merely circles the number of each voter as he comes in to cast his ballot.

The newly arrived voter signs the poll book as identification, and the deputy then hands him a folded ballot paper bearing the deputy's initials, and with a numbered counterfoil attached.

The voter takes his ballot to the booth and marks his choice by making a simple cross with the black lead pencil, according to the instructions prominently posted in the polling station. A ballot marked in any other way may be rejected at the count.

After the voter has marked his ballot, he refolds it so that his choice remains secret, brings it out of the booth, and hands it to the deputy, who, in the presence of the voter, tears off the counterfoil and puts the ballot through the narrow slot of the box.

Early in the day, the scrutineer should cast his own ballot if he has not already voted at the advance poll. If he happens to be registered in a different poll from the one in which he is scrutineering, the election-day manager will have obtained from the returning officer or election clerk a transfer certificate entitling the scrutineer to vote instead at the polling station where he is scrutineering.

As the day goes on, the scrutineer should take an occasional look into the booth or booths, to remove any political literature which may have been left there by voters. He might check for broken pencils at the same time; if the pencil is broken, voters will be tempted to use their own pens, and ballots marked in ink may not be counted.

There are a few circumstances for which special procedures are laid down. If a voter accidentally mismarks his ballot, he may invalidate it by putting a cross against all the candidates' names, and exchange it for a new ballot with the deputy returning officer. An illiterate or incapacitated voter, after making application under oath, can have his ballot marked by the deputy returning officer in the presence of the poll clerk and the scrutineers. A blind voter can take a friend into the voting booth to mark his ballot slip for him.

THE OUTSIDE SCRUTINEER   There should be an outside scrutineer for each poll. He regularly visits the polling station to get up-to-the-minute information from the inside scrutineer; but most of his time is spent outside. His main task is to get out the vote.

The outside scrutineer's kit should include:
(a) credentials to enable him to enter the polling station;
(b) written instructions;
(c) a poll book accurately marked with the final results of the canvassing, to show definite supporters and possible supporters;
(d) a large-scale map of the poll;
(e) a pen or pencil and a scratchpad;
(f) a non-partisan poll badge. The badge will identify him to the inside scrutineer when he enters

the polling station. The inside scrutineer would not want to give out his valuable records to an unknown person.

A candidate is entitled to have as many scrutineers as he wishes; but there should not be more than 2 of them in the polling station at any one time.

The outside scrutineer needs a convenient place, near the polling station, where he can write, make phone calls, and have someone on duty all day to answer the phone. This may well be in the living room of some supporter near by. Perhaps he can share this mini-headquarters with another outside scrutineer from the neighbouring poll. With luck, the outside scrutineer may have a car and driver at his disposal all day; but often transportation arrangements are centralized at the main constituency committee room.

Here is a good procedure for the outside scrutineer. Like the inside scrutineer, he must be sworn in as an agent of the candidate. Unless he has already voted at the advance poll, he then casts his ballot, in his own poll if that is where he is working, otherwise by transfer certificate.

About once an hour he calls at the polling station to obtain from his inside scrutineer the numbers of the people who have already voted. He then transfers those numbers to his own records. If the outside scrutineer has also been the election canvasser, he knows his poll well, and knows who to phone early and who to phone late, in order to remind them to come out and vote. He does not wish to antagonize voters, but if he does not start this task early, he will be snowed under by poll-closing time.

The outside scrutineer will continually assess his poll throughout the day. He might approach a supporter over the telephone, or he might call personally: "Good afternoon. I represent Candidate James Smith. Today is election day, and I would like to remind you that the polls close at 7 p.m. You vote at 3030 Comox Street. I hope you and your wife will be able to vote early. May I offer you a ride to the polling station?"

Most city polls are within easy walking distance, so most voters will refuse the ride; but offering it is a useful gesture. If they tell you what time they are going to vote, you make a note of this.

Where a mother has young children to care for, the outside scrutineer will provide a babysitter. When elderly people require a ride, the outside scrutineer will provide a car and driver.

Often a voter will not know where to vote, so he will solve the problem by asking his favourite political party for a ride to the poll. The unusually shrewd voter will phone the opponent for a ride.

If the outside scrutineer has a good rapport with his neighbourhood, the job is easy and pleasant. I remember serving as inside scrutineer in an election in Vancouver Centre in a poll with the usual 250 to 300 voters. The outside scrutineer had been a canvasser in that poll for about six weeks. He had canvassed it three times and had clearly identified our supporters. He told me that we would win that poll by 60 percent. I said I did not believe him. He replied that it was my job to look after the inside of the polling station, and that he would manage the outside of the poll without any interference from me. After the count I found out that his projections were right.

If the outside scrutineer is a stranger to the poll, his job is somewhat more difficult, but it is no less important.

THE COUNT At closing time, the outside door of the polling station is locked; but everybody who is inside by that time is entitled to vote. When the last ballot has been cast, the poll is closed. Then the deputy returning officer is required to follow this procedure:

(a) Seal the slot of the ballot box.

(b) Count the number of voters who have signed the poll book.

(c) Count the returned, mismarked ballot papers, if any.

(d) Check the number of new ballot papers issued in exchange for mismarked ones.

(e) Count the unused ballot papers.

(f) Open the ballot box, count the votes, and record on tally sheets the number of votes given for each candidate.

(g) Count any rejected ballots.

(h) Account for all ballot papers.

There are 2 steps of this procedure that should be described in some detail.

The ballot-box lid must be opened in the presence of the poll clerk and the inside scrutineers. If the candidates or parties have no appointed scrutineers, then any 2 registered voters may act as witnesses; indeed, the deputy returning officer may not begin the count without 2 witnesses, in addition to himself and the poll clerk.

I like the procedure in which the deputy returning officer turns the box upside down on a big table and dumps all the ballots out. Everybody looks into the box to make sure it is empty. Then the deputy returning officer sorts the ballot slips into piles. If there are 4 candidates he will have 5 piles; the extra pile is for ballot slips which he believes should be rejected. He is supposed to reject any ballot papers that

(a) Have not been supplied by him;

(b) Have not been properly marked with a cross in the small circular space;

(c) Have been marked for too many candidates;

(d) Can be identified by any unusual writing or mark.

In close contests, rejected ballots can win or lose elections, so a scrutineer should look closely at ballots rejected by the deputy returning officer, and argue vigorously for acceptance of any which contain a vote for his own candidate. This is quite legitimate; scrutineers are present as partisans, not as impartial judges.

A good returning officer can finish the counting in about an hour and a half. Next he must give a written statement of the results to each scrutineer. Then he completes the rest of his paperwork, which is considerable, puts his materials back in the ballot box, reseals the lid, and delivers the box to his constituency returning officer. He should keep out of the box a written statement of the results and his expense account, and deliver those 2 items separately to the returning officer.

The steps that I have described in this chapter have been taken from the federal elections act; but the procedure changes somewhat from one jurisdiction to another.

BACK AT THE COMMITTEE ROOM

Back at the committee room a lot of supporters, and probably the candidate too, are waiting to hear the results of the voting. When the polls have closed, everybody is asked to keep off the telephone, so that the inside scrutineers from the different polls can phone in their results to headquarters. As soon as a scrutineer at a polling station receives his official statement of the results, he telephones it to the committee room. He should first give his poll number, then read the number of votes for the candidates—in the same order as they are on the ballot.

After phoning, the scrutineer takes that written statement, as fast as he can, to the committee room. All those written statements of results should be preserved, in case a recount is needed.

As each scrutineer's telephoned report comes in, an election worker writes the figures on a chit of paper, repeats them for accuracy, then hands the chit to a board-marker. The headquarters-hall manager has already arranged for a large board, covered with white paper and divided into sections for polls and candidates, to be hung on the wall. Usually the votes from each poll go across horizontally and the individual candidates' totals run vertically. For example:

COUNTING BOARD

Poll No.	Lib.	NDP	P. Con.	Socred
1				
2	76	(84)	10	72
3				
4	70	98	(121)	46

The board-marker writes the scores on the board as he gets the results from the telephone operator. A number of adding machines, one for each candidate, keep a running total, which is posted on a second board.

It is a time of great suspense. Sometimes arithmetical errors result in candidates' and managers' dying and reviving again between 8 p.m. and 10 p.m. If your candidate finally wins, a party follows. The victory party is one feature of the campaign that seems never to require any planning.

I remember one election night at Powell River, B.C., an arithmetical error was made. The daily press added an extra zero to the total of the Conservative candidate; even that bonus still left him in third place. On day two after the election, a commentator devoted a whole program to the resurgence of the Conservative party in Mackenzie and the reasons for such a development. I did not bother to correct the error; the election was over.

CHECKLISTS   INSIDE SCRUTINEERS

1. If possible, read in advance Sections 36 to 42 of the *Canada Elections Act*.
2. Meet your outside scrutineer at a training session.
3. With equipment and credentials, attend the designated poll 45 minutes before it opens. Present credentials and get sworn in.

4. Vote at your own poll, or through a transfer certificate, or at the advance poll.
5. On a copy of the voters' list, mark off each voter as he signs the poll book.
6. Note voters' numbers on poll slips; give these to the outside scrutineer when he visits.
7. Unless relieved, stay at your poll for the count.
8. Be provided with a description of a valid ballot.
9. Contest rejected ballots that could be votes for your candidate.
10. Have telephone number of committee room handy and phone in the results.

OUTSIDE SCRUTINEERS
1. Meet your inside scrutineer at a training session.
2. Find in advance a local headquarters, near the polling station, for use on election day.
3. Have a list of positive and possible supporters for your assigned poll.
4. Have written instructions for election day, including telephone number of central committee room.
5. On election day, vote early before you start work if you have not voted at the advance poll.
6. Present credentials to deputy returning officer of your poll; get sworn in so you can come and go in the poll at will.
7. Regularly collect poll slips from the inside scrutineer; check on your own list supporters who have voted.
8. Throughout the day, call on supporters who have not voted:
   (a) Persuade them to vote early.
   (b) Where necessary, arrange rides or babysitting with poll-based or centralized services.
9. If there is trouble in the poll, relay messages from the inside scrutineer to the central committee room.
10. If no inside scrutineer is available, just before closing time enter the poll and remain for the count.

11. Remember that, for polling day, you have the most important role in the election. Getting 1 or 2 extra supporters to the poll can bring victory to your candidate.

14 After the Election

HOW TO BE A MONDAY-MORNING QUARTERBACK.

I described in Chapter 13 how scrutineers at the polls rapidly phone their results to the committee rooms. Within seconds these figures are posted on the scoreboards, and the newsmen present are phoning those totals to their editorial rooms.

The campaign manager, the candidate, and other knowledgeable election workers will have already studied the political history of the riding back over several elections and will know which polls best indicate the general trend.

If one candidate has a long lead over the others, his victory will soon be apparent. In a typical provincial or federal election, the unofficial results are usually known 2 or 3 hours after the polls close.

The deputy returning officers, who have more paperwork to do, are a little slower getting their results in to the constituency returning officer. But by midnight, the whole process is over, and morning newspapers will tell a province or the nation the results in detail.

PRAISE AND BLAME

About 11 p.m. on an election night, the candidate makes a statement to his supporters. This moment is critical. If you have won, you must thank your workers and be gracious to the losers. If you are a loser, you must congratulate the winner. It need be only a private phone-call, but it should definitely be done. At this time the candidate must be gracious. A candidate who shows himself generous in defeat is taking the first step towards victory in another election, and a bitter, angry, losing candidate comes across very badly on television.

At this moment the campaign manager is in a no-win position. If your party has won, the candidate gets the glory; if you lose, the campaign manager gets the blame—an inevitable result of the pressure the campaign manager has had to apply to everybody to get the job done. The candidate should give a word of special thanks to this key member of the campaign team.

CLEANING UP   The next day, clean up your campaign headquarters before handing them over to the landlord. But don't throw out all the old papers with the empty beer bottles; save carefully all material that can be used for the next election: supporters' names, addresses, and phone numbers, sample copies of workers' instructions, and all kinds of campaign literature. Also save several copies of the voters' list. The candidate will find this list useful for contacting his constituents; party organizers, too, can use the information for organizing drives between elections.

Lawn signs should be promptly retrieved. Whether the candidate has won or lost, supporters do not like yesterday's election sign sitting in their front gardens. The plywood sheets, posts, nuts, and bolts can be stored in a basement ready for the next campaign.

No less important is the financial clean-up. It damages the reputation of your candidate and your party if you leave printers' or newspapers' bills unpaid. If you are unable to pay all debts immediately, your whole executive should march to the bank and co-sign for a loan.

OFFICIAL   The candidate and the official agent should attend on
DUTIES   the returning officer for the official addition of votes, held soon after polling day. In British Columbia this procedure is called the final count. At this time the

ballot boxes are opened, the statements of polls from the deputy returning officers are added up, and the returning officer declares the winning candidate. The ballot bundles are *not* opened and recounted at this stage. Unless someone obtains a court order to have a judge recount the ballots and reassess the rejected or spoiled ballot papers, the count made in the excitement of election night is the final count.

The successful candidate is entitled to a written statement from the returning officer, declaring him to be the winner.

Often, all this is only a formality, but if the result is very close, this official addition, or final count, is of some strategic significance. The *Canada Elections Act* prescribes that applications for a recount must be made within 4 days after the date on which the returning officer has declared the name of the winning candidate. So if your candidate has lost by 100 votes or less, he and his supporters may consider an application to the court for a recount; for this, they must read their *Elections Act*, and draw up affidavits giving sufficient facts to convince a judge to order a recount.

The campaign committee will then meet to wind up its affairs. After that dissolution, the constituency executive will resume its former authority and responsibility; it will begin to analyse the election that has just passed and prepare for the one to come.

ACCOUNTS AND THANKS   Win or lose, soon after the election the candidate must furnish his statement of personal expenses to the official agent, so that the agent can, in turn, transmit it to the returning officer. Those expenses will later be published in a newspaper at the expense of the candidate.

In addition to this official report to the returning officer, your organization should make an accurate financial report to your contributors. Any political party which has a broad financial base must offer such a careful accounting to preserve its credibility. Get this accounting done as fast as you can, because you should be able to enclose a brief financial statement, plus the official receipts for income-tax purposes, if applicable, along with the thank-you letters.

As soon as possible after election day, the candidate, the campaign manager, and the official agent must sit down and draft a thank-you letter to all who have assisted in the campaign. The candidate should sign all those letters personally, even if it takes several hours or several evenings. No matter how cheaply the text of the letter itself is duplicated, that personal signature will be appreciated by your supporters.

The candidate should also make a few telephone calls to thank personally the key people in his campaign. He should also follow up his thank-you letters with Christmas cards, or anniversary cards one year later, to show his people that he has not forgotten them.

Here are drafts of thank-you letters suitable for campaign managers and candidates.

Date: Constituency:
                               Address:
                               Phone Number:

Dear Miss Brown:

Thank you for the help you gave us in the last federal election. We enclose a copy of our election expenses and your official receipt for an election contribution, to be used when filing your income-tax return. We ended the campaign with a surplus of $103.

Bob Smith, our candidate, did a great job, and had we started the campaign a little earlier we would have done better at the polls. Some of us are asking Bob Smith to run again four years from now, because we think our party can win this riding.

We are holding a coffee party on January 20, 1978, at 2 p.m. for Grace Smith, the national leader, at the above address. Bob Smith will act as chairman.

We would especially like to see you at the coffee party.

We have some coloured slides of the campaign you might like to see, as well as meet old friends again. Thanks.

Yours truly,
SIGNATURE
Campaign Manager

(Campaign manager should sign personally in ink.)

Date: Constituency:
                         Address:
                         Phone Number:

Dear Mr. Jones:

Thank you for the help you gave us in the last provincial election. It was a thrill to see so many people like yourself making democracy work. I enclose a condensed copy of campaign expenses from the official agent and the final count results from the returning officer.

We increased our winning vote slightly and ended the campaign with a financial surplus of $98.

We are going to have a get-together party in a short while and will be contacting you. We will be showing coloured slides and our scrapbook of the campaign. Thanks again.

Kindest personal regards,
SIGNATURE

(Candidate should sign personally in ink.)

THE WINNER The winning candidate's first formal duty will be to be sworn in to his newly won office. The swearing-in ceremony is usually colourful, and the new member should try to obtain photographs of it. These photographs will be useful for publicity in the dog days before the new session gets started.

REPORTING Whatever office he holds, it is important that the
BACK election-winner should report back regularly to his constituents. Ronald Basford, MP for Vancouver Centre, sends a written report through the mail about twice a year. Once he sent me with his report a blank

cheque made out to the Ron Basford Liberal Campaign Headquarters, with a business-reply envelope affixed to the cheque so that I could easily mail it back as a campaign contribution.

Once a year, when the legislature had finished its work, it was my practice to travel up and down the coast within the boundaries of the Mackenzie riding. I would plot my journey by steamer, automobile, or plane, endeavouring to spend two or three days in each locality.

When I was first elected to the legislature in 1952, my indemnity was $3,000 a year, plus about $100 a year for travel expenses. In those days we had to pay our own postage.

People were always complaining that I did not come around often enough; that was true, but it was not easy to solve the problem. On those early trips around the riding, I was careful to advertise in the local papers that I was holding legislative report meetings, and that the public was welcome. In fact, not many people came; but most did see the ads, knew that I was in the district, and were pleased that I had been around. There is no point in a member's visiting the neighbourhood if no one knows he is there.

Most members write weekly columns for their local and ethnic press. My attitude towards the media was to try and be genuinely helpful. Donald Lockstead, MLA, the present member for Mackenzie, telephones the Powell River radio station once a week with a report of sessional business; it is undoubtedly recorded, and broadcast at convenient times over CHQB.

Garry Lauk, MLA, and Emery Barnes, MLA, regularly report through mimeographed circulars from Victoria to their supporters in the provincial riding of Vancouver Centre. Not only should a member do good things, but he must make sure that his constituents know what he has done.

Yet there are limits. Some federal MPs from Western Canada return from Ottawa to their constituencies once a week. This severe strain is not in the interest of the members of Parliament, or of the public.

I would like to point out, too, that this reporting process should work both ways. If you feel that your member is doing a good job, or has helped you, write him a note. He will appreciate it.

THE LOSERS   A first-time candidate who has been hard-working and honest need not fret about losing an election; if he has conducted himself well, he will likely be asked to run again for some office in the same constituency. And the next time it will be easier. The candidate will have made a name for himself in the first contest, and will have a few newspaper clippings to base his new campaign on. He will also have saved some newspaper clippings about his opponent, for possible comment in the future; and he will also have saved the other side's campaign literature so as to keep a careful tally of promises made and promises broken.

POST-ELECTION   Regardless of the election results, the campaign
STUDY   manager and the candidate should both write reports showing what they think went right, and wrong, with the campaign. The two separate reports are useful because they usually, and understandably, give two different points of view. Several months later, when the official returns are published by the Chief Electoral Officer, academically minded members of the organization will gladly volunteer to do a deeper assessment of the long-range political implications of the results.

Right through the campaign, the official historian will have been gathering material; he can now be systematically pasting it into a big scrapbook. In this book should go all relevant newspaper clippings, samples of all printed literature (front and back) issued by yourself and your opponents, and every mimeographed letter or handwritten note which the historian can lay his hands on. The historian will have taken many photographs, too, for the scrapbook. Every item will be dated, as accurately as possible.

All of this recording, reporting, and analysing is part of the vitally important long-term process of preparing, far in advance, for the next election. For municipal elections, the plan can be quite specific, because the dates of those elections are usually established by statute, every 2 years. Federal and provincial elections are usually held every 4 years, but may be somewhat earlier or later, according to the judgment of the first minister concerned. By-elections, of course, may occur at any time.

Politicians who wish to be prepared in the event of an election should set up permanent election machinery. It is not difficult. You can appoint a campaign chairman and a small committee to do the planning at leisure. Here are the minimum preparations required.

1. Appoint a campaign chairman.
2. Draw up a critical path plan.
3. Prepare the design, but not the text, of a basic leaflet.
4. Prepare the basic design for a poster 11" x 14" (approx. 28 cm x 35 cm).
5. Prepare basic designs for street signs 4' x 8' (approx. 1200 cm x 2400 cm).
6. Prepare instructions for inside scrutineers.
7. Prepare instructions for outside scrutineers.
8. Prepare instructions for canvassers.
9. Prepare canvassers' poll books.
10. Draft written instructions for chairmen of subcommittees.
11. Get a copy of the last voters' list.
12. Draft the campaign budget.
13. Draft a sample fund-raising letter.
14. Get a copy of the relevant *Elections Act*.
15. If the riding is a large one geographically, or if your candidate is a party leader, you should also plan a tentative speaking itinerary for him.

Elections in Associations and Clubs

DEMOCRACY CLOSE TO HOME.

The strategy and tactics that I have been presenting for use in municipal, provincial, and federal elections can be applied, with suitable modifications, everywhere that elections are held. They can be used in community associations, parent-teacher associations, artistic and philanthropic societies—in all organizations where people combine for a common purpose within some kind of democratic structure. Look at the number of entries under "Clubs" and "Associations" in the Yellow Pages of a phone book. In most of these, elections are being regularly held; members are voting, or not voting; executives are setting policy, raising money, spending money, influencing the lives of their own members, of their members' families, and, often, of other people too. These organizations are, to a noticeable extent, shaping the society in which we live.

This book is about winning elections, so let us consider an imaginary situation in which you and some of your friends are members of some organization, be it a professional society or a bowling league. You feel that the present leadership has failed to carry out the aims of the organization, or perhaps the present executive is undemocratic, ignoring the desires of the members. For one reason or another, it is time for a change, and you and some other

members feel qualified to make that change. Here are
the major points to consider and to act on.

DEFINE POLICY   A new candidate seeking office in any kind of
organization needs someone to consult with.
Consultation is the key to wise, effective policy
formation. So ask people to help you. The act of
asking people to help you is, in fact, the beginning of
your campaign.

One of the first things to do is to form a policy
committee. It does not much matter whether or not
you formally call that group a "policy committee"; the
important point is that it should meet regularly to
create and to evaluate new policy ideas. For this
purpose the committee should be truly representative
of the organization, proportionately balanced by sex,
age group, race, technical skill, or any other qualities
that are significant in the organization. A community
arts-council, for example, may be headed for trouble
if all the members of its policy committee are
symphony-concert fans.

Here are a few general principles for use in this
process of policy formation. First, remember that
criticism by itself is not policy. There may be many
things wrong with the policy of the present executive,
perhaps with the organization as a whole; but while
"Throw the rascals out" may, in some circumstances,
be a useful slogan, it is not adequate as a statement of
policy. A good policy must be predominantly
positive.

For example, when trying to organize a group of
workers into a union for the first time, it is not
enough to tell them what a villain the boss is; you
have to define for those potential members the precise
benefits they may expect to win through union
membership.

Also, policy changes should not be too radical, too
abrupt; you cannot afford to dissociate yourself from
everything the old executive has done and everything
the membership has previously accepted. Nor can you
seriously hope to turn all of them about-face and set

them marching briskly off in a completely new direction. A prudent candidate and policy committee will utilize whatever is good and useful in the old policy, and will preserve and build on that, while trying over the long term, like a good teacher, to overcome whatever is negative and harmful.

To sum up, then, your policy needs something of the old, plus a sprinkling of the new, and should be built around the established virtues of your organization. This policy development cannot properly be done in one quick session held a week or ten days before the annual meetings. Like political policy-building, it should be started far in advance; at least 6 months in advance for an organization that has annual elections.

The new policy, when it is finally worked out, must then be communicated to the voting members. Here, as in politics, I recommend getting the proposed policy clearly and concisely printed on leaflets not bigger than one sheet of letter-size paper. In a small organization where all, or nearly all, the members meet regularly, the policy leaflets can be handed out at meetings. For larger organizations, mail distribution may be better.

Years ago, I remember, in elections for the executive of Local 1-217 of the International Woodworkers of America, we published policy leaflets in the several languages spoken by our members, most of whom were employed in sawmills throughout the city of Vancouver.

Analysis of existing policies, and the creation, where necessary, of new policy must be kept up all the time, not only until the election, but also after victory, if you wish to hold the position you have won. Under Richard J. Daley of Chicago the poll captains in the city were full-time employees of City Hall. When each poll captain left his home in the morning, he was expected to allow himself twenty or thirty minutes extra in walking to his car or transit stop. The neighbours knew that the poll captain took that walk every morning, so they could conveniently stop him and tell him what they thought was right or wrong with the city government, or ask assistance from City Hall for some of their troubles.

In a trade union, a potential executive member should have as many shop stewards as possible on his side, and not on the side of the opponents.

The same principle applies in any organization: a good president and a good executive will not be satisfied with discussing business among themselves; they will devise some system for keeping a finger on the pulse of the general membership. Even the old-fashioned suggestions box, placed near the door at every meeting, will likely yield some very instructive ideas.

CANDIDATES   There is no such thing as an ideal candidate; that holds true for non-political as well as political organizations. The practical procedure is to choose, far ahead of time, the best candidate you can find for president or chairman, and the best group of candidates for the executive posts, and then stay with them all the way, right up to the election and through the ensuing year, or years, of activity. If you cannot give a candidate that full, lasting support, then it may be that you need another candidate. Here are qualities to look for.

1. Does he share the interests of the membership, and does he understand the purposes of the organization? Candidates for office should always be respected for their knowledge or attainments in the relevant fields of activity. If you are seeking candidacy, are you thus qualified? If not, can you make yourself qualified in time for the next, or next-but-one, election?

2. Nobodies do not get elected. Has the potential candidate already made himself visible, or can he quickly make himself visible within the organization? Can he create for himself, among the members, a reputation for activity, reliability, competence?

Achieving visibility is not difficult for anyone who can deliver an acceptable speech. Make a point of standing up once or twice at every business meeting to debate an issue or comment on a policy.

Volunteer for necessary tasks and do them well, whether it be organizing the annual picnic or tournament, running a drive for funds, or renovating the clubroom. When the job is done, write a detailed report, so that when the same occasion comes around next time, a future organizer will benefit from your experience and remember your name.

Take advantage of the regular meetings. Try to be the first person there. Chat with your fellow members, open a few doors, set out a few chairs, or pour a few cups of coffee. Make sure that you have time to talk to people, and that you have the patience to let people talk to you. A good candidate is a good listener. Never leave the meeting early. Wait till all the business has been concluded; stay behind and, if necessary, help clean up the clubroom. Then invite some members to your home for coffee and a sandwich.

3. The most powerful weapon any candidate has is his own home and his own family. A big house, a charming spouse, and several children form a public-relations system that is hard to beat. For wise selection of candidates, do not depend solely on formal committee meetings and ballots. Whether you are seeking nomination yourself, or are sizing up other people as potential candidates for office, a house party, a dinner, or a barbecue provide excellent means of getting to know people. While you do not need to plan discussions of policy or election strategy at such affairs, the social gathering gives friends and neighbours the chance to question you on current issues—if they wish; it also gives potential allies the chance to become better acquainted. There is certainly no need for elaborate entertainment on such occasions; all that is required is that the guests be well chosen and the host gracious.

COALITIONS   As a general rule, the new contender for office in any organization starts off in a minority position, so he must form a coalition to strengthen his forces. One might say that a contender has to go looking for friends. Suppose you are doing just that; and suppose that a respected member of the organization says, "Yes, I will help you in your campaign against the old guard, provided that I get a position on your slate."

In other words, this member will lend his influence and his personal activity to your campaign if he is guaranteed a seat on the executive, a trip as delegate to the next convention, or something like that.

Persons who cannot establish coalitions and hold them together cannot win elections. In politics the process is called log-rolling. Successful coalitions achieve victory and preserve stability.

THE SLATE   The word *slate* acquired its political sense in 1877, in the United States. That political sense derives from the older meaning of the word, "a thin, flat, rectangular piece of slate mounted in a wooden frame". You can write clearly on it with a piece of chalk and, no less important, you can erase instantly with one wipe of a rag. Nowadays nominating meetings commonly use a blackboard, but the final list of nominees is still called a slate. The very use of the word implies that there will be opposition in the election and, quite likely, an opposition slate.

When a contest arises in an association, there are usually several members of an executive to elect, plus a president or chairman. You will need to choose from the people you believe to be eligible. Obviously qualified would be those who have helped you in the preliminary organization, and so have proved their ability to work hard and harmoniously. Then it is usually wise to put forward for the executive some-thing of a mixture—a few wise old heads, a few young Turks—somewhat along the lines that I rec-ommended for the policy committee.

But it is not enough to work out this model executive on the blackboard at the nominating meeting. You cannot expect large numbers of ordinary members to memorize all those names; so you must get them down in print, and distribute copies to your supporters at or before the election. Most people welcome this leadership.

The custom is to print the slate on a sheet small enough to slip easily into a breast pocket or purse.

VOTING
PROCEDURES

Where more than one person is to be elected on one ballot, you should warn your own supporters to be careful not to vote your opponents into office. Here is a simple example. Suppose that there are two posts to be filled on the executive of Ourtown Cultural Society. There are three candidates, Messrs. Goode, Middling, and Rotten. You are supporting one person, namely Goode. You have assessed the members' feelings, as well as you can. Middling has rather weak support; Rotten has a pretty strong backing, but you think you could just about beat him in a two-way contest.

But this is a three-way contest. A lot of Rotten's supporters may give their second votes to Middling, and vice versa. A lot of your supporters may also vote for Middling, with the idea that at least he is better than Rotten. The net result could be that Middling comes in an easy winner, Rotten comes in second, and Goode is left in the losing third place.

The golden rule for such multi-place elections must be "Vote only for the person(s) on your slate, and not for anyone else at all."

This technique is called *plumping*. It applies just as well if you have a slate of four candidates running for seven vacant positions. Well-directed plumping can be a powerful tactic and is often used by minority groups to get at least a few people on the executive. They concentrate their voting strength on their own slate members, and are not foolish enough to vote for their opponents under any circumstances.

Some organizations try to prevent plumping by various anti-plumping by-laws. One example: each party or faction that wants to put up any candidate at all must file a full slate; so if there are seven positions to be filled, you have to produce seven bodies to fill them. This technique could, I suppose, be called keeping your supporters in your political corral; it stops their votes from spilling over onto other people's slates and helping to elect your opponents.

Another kind of anti-plumping rule is that if seven positions are open, each voter must cast seven votes; he is not allowed, for example, to vote for just the five candidates whom he really likes. Under this rule, any ballot containing less than the full number of votes is declared spoiled, and none of that member's votes will count at all.

I have never approved of anti-plumping by-laws. I feel that a member of an association should be free to vote for just those candidates that he wishes, without being forced to vote for others whom he does not honestly support.

People who deliberately do not vote the full slate are called *ticket-splitters*. They are the bane of well-established groups within an organization, but those ticket-splitters are often receptive to the campaign efforts of independents. Many a minority candidate has ridden to victory on the votes of the ticket-splitters.

GETTING OUT THE VOTE   Getting your supporters to the election is just as important at the annual meeting of the chess club or the trade union as it is in a national parliamentary election. Supporters who sit at home on election night are not of any use to the individual candidate or to the slate.

There is no need to hesitate; people want to help, and they enjoy being asked to help. Quite likely nobody in the organization has ever before asked them to help. So phone a few friends the day before the meeting, tell them you want their support, and explain why you want it. Offer them a ride to the meeting, or perhaps a ride home from the meeting; but one way or another, get your supporters to that meeting in time for the election.

It is simple enough, getting your supporters out to vote, but it is the essential final feature of your campaign. If one side is doing it and the other side is not, the slate that gets out the vote wins the election. Even if you only bring out three or four people, they may provide your margin of victory.

SECRECY   It sometimes happens that an organization, apparently running on democratic principles, is in fact under the control of an inner circle, or clique. The general membership does not suspect what is going on, but only sees the results, a well-oiled mechanism clicking over at the time of the annual meeting, a show of debating and voting, but in reality little or no power in the hands of the voter-members.

It is possible that some of the executive members are not aware of the situation. Suppose you are attending an executive meeting of your association, and gradually get the impression that important chunks of the meeting have been rehearsed, that the present session seems like a second run-through. Then, quite possibly, those parts of the meeting have indeed been rehearsed—when the predominant group caucused prior to the main meeting.

Such a clique may use a secret slate as a tool for making election results come out the way they want. Years ago my brother, Herbert Gargrave, arrived at a constituency meeting and found, to his annoyance, that there was just one slate of delegates to the convention, and that he was not on it. On a point of privilege he obtained the floor and denounced the secret opposition-slate as an attempt to interfere with the democratic process. As he spoke he waved the secret slate in the air and read out the names, so as to identify and isolate the opposition and give leadership to his own supporters not to vote for that slate. At the next election my brother had his own slate.

It is always important to be on guard against any form of underground campaigning. Watch for signs of such activity. When you are sure of your facts, and have some corroborative evidence, your candidate should go on the attack, expose the campaign, offer his corroborative documents, or a supporting speaker, and let the association make its own judgment.

Underground techniques can be highly effective, so long as the general membership does not know what is going on, but publicity will generally win the day. It is best that the by-laws of your organization provide, as far as possible, for all executive decisions, nominations, slates, and campaign activity to be made known to the general membership. That way everyone knows who stands for what.

FOREWARNED
IS FOREARMED

Readers may feel that some of the advice I have offered in this chapter is Machiavellian. Perhaps, but they should keep in mind that a candidate who does not know these techniques will be at the mercy of an opponent who does.

How these methods will be used depends on the character and good sense of the aspiring candidate and his supporters. If the supporters sincerely want to further the aims of the organization, if the candidate works diligently and uses a few well-tried, vote-getting techniques, then they have good prospects of winning the election.

SUMMARY OF
SUCCESSFUL
TECHNIQUES

1. Good candidates are:
   (a) Capable, respected members.
   (b) Able to achieve high visibility.
   (c) In general, good citizens.
   (d) Skilled at informal activities.
2. Well-defined policy:
   (a) Form a representative policy committee.
   (b) Communicate policy to members.
   (c) Get, and analyse, members' reactions.
3. A strong slate:
   (a) Get a good assortment of candidates.
   (b) Print sufficient copies.
4. Correct voting procedures:
   (a) Be sure, yourself, of prescribed procedures.
   (b) Give accurate instructions to supporters.
5. Get out your vote: easy but essential.
6. Coalition: form it early; keep it together.
7. Be aware of caucus operations in your organization.

Conclusion

Good organization is the key to the success of any campaign. If you take the time and trouble to organize your campaign carefully, define your strategy and tactics, and then select competent individuals to carry them out, you will conduct a responsible and efficient campaign.

I have refrained from advocating any political programs or policies in this book. My main purpose has been to provide a comprehensive guide to organizing and running *any* election campaign; the principles of sound organization and clear thinking apply wherever democratic elections are held.

If, after reading *How To Win an Election*, the reader has a greater understanding of the Canadian political system and a feeling of the potential of his own contribution, I will feel that this book has achieved its purpose.

SAMPLE CRITICAL PATH PLAN

DAYS TO ELECTION

43|42|41|40|39|38|37|36|35|34|33|32|31|30|29|28|27|26|25|24|23|22|21|20|19|18|17|16|15|14|13|12|11|10|9|8|7|6|5|4|3|2|1|0|-1

NOVEMBER

28|29|30|31|1|2|3|4|5|6|7|8|9|10|11|12|13|14|15|16|17|18|19|20|21|22|23|24|25|26|27|28|29|30

DECEMBER

1|2|3|4|5|6|7|8|9|10|11

Candidates' Meeting

Finalize Budget

Letter to Editor

Approve Leaflet and Advertising

Print General Leaflet

Nominate Candidate
(Holiday)

Put Up Signs

Start Canvass

Distribute Leaflet(s)

Complete Distribution of Leaflet(s)
Put Bumper-Stickers Up

Mail Slate Cards

Public Meeting

Election Day

Assess Results and Mail Thank-You Notes

[·] DAILY NEWSPAPER ADS

▶ SYMBOLIC PEAKING OF CAMPAIGN

Candidate's Diary

This Diary presents the duties of a candidate and his official agent in the order that they should be performed. It may be helpful to place a check mark beside each item as it is completed.

(a) PRELIMINARY STEPS

(1) If entitled to do so, *nominate*:

Sec. 18 ☐
Schedule A
Rules (1)-(7);
(65)-(71)

- *urban enumerators*—one for each urban polling division in the electoral district prior to twelve o'clock noon, on the 54th day before polling day.

☐

- *urban revising agents*—one for each revisal district in the electoral district.

The two candidates who at the previous election received the highest number of votes are required to nominate enumerators and revising agents for appointment by the returning officer. The returning officer must notify these candidates when the nominations are to be made. Each person nominated must be qualified as an elector in the electoral district and must be a fit and proper person.

Sec. 18(3) ☐ (2) Inspect the lists of names of urban and rural enumerators posted in the office of the returning officer.

(3) As soon as his candidacy is declared, make the following appointments:

Sec. 62(1)   ☐   • *official agent.* The candidate's campaign should not begin before the appointment of his official agent.

Sec. 62.1(1) ☐   • *auditor.* The auditor must be appointed at the same time as the official agent.

☐   (4) Report to the returning officer as soon as possible:
  • the name, address, and occupation of his official agent
  • the name and address of his auditor.

☐   (5) To enable his offical agent to properly manage the election campaign, notify his supporters at once of that appointment.

Sec. 19(7)   ☐   (6) Receive five copies of the election Proclamation from the returning officer.

(7) Obtain from the returning officer:

☐   • copies of this Manual

☐   • indexed copies of the *Canada Elections Act*

☐   • copies of the nomination paper (comprising forms 27, 28, 29 and 30).

(b) OFFICIAL NOMINATION

A candidate cannot stand for election unless he becomes *officially nominated* by filing his nomination paper with the returning officer. Section 23 of the Act sets out the procedure for the official nomination of a candidate.

The date of nomination is declared in the election Proclamation and is normally:

Sec. 22(5,8)   • at a general election, Monday, the 21st day before polling day (except in an electoral district listed in Schedule III to the Act)

Sec. 106(b)   • at a by-election, Monday, the 14th day before polling day (except in an electoral district listed in Schedule III to the Act)

Sec. 22(5,8)   • at a general election or by-election in one of the electoral districts listed in Schedule III to the Act, Monday, the 28th day before polling day.

Sec. 23   ☐   (1) Complete and submit the official nomination paper.

A candidate's nomination paper may be filed with the returning officer at any time after the date of the election Proclamation, but no later than 2 p.m. on nomination day. A candidate is strongly advised to file his nomination paper as early as possible.

A nomination paper must be signed by each of 25 or more qualified electors in the electoral district, in the presence of a witness. It must show the name, address, and occupation of the candidate's official agent and the name and address of the candidate's auditor.

When a nomination paper is handed to the returning officer, it must be accompanied by a deposit of $200 (legal tender or certified cheque) and a letter of endorsement, if any, from a registered party. A letter of endorsement entitles a candidate to have his party's name printed underneath his name on the ballot paper. Otherwise, the ballot paper will show the word "independent", unless the candidate requests in writing that no description be shown. People who have signed a nomination paper as witnesses must take an oath before the returning officer at the time that the paper is filed.

(2) After the nomination paper is filed, obtain from the returning officer the following:

Sec. 23(8) ☐ • the returning officer's receipt, which is a candidate's proof that he has been officially nominated.

☐ • copies of Book 1—"Candidate's Journal of Receipts Issued for Income Tax Purposes" and a copy of Book 2—"Candidate's Revenue and Expenses".

☐ • sufficient copies—two for each polling station in the electoral district—of the form for appointing an agent of the candidate (poll agent) (form 100).

☐ • copies of the forms for the "Candidate's Return Respecting Election Expenses" and the candidate's

"Declaration Respecting Election Expenses".
(comprising forms 64, 65, 66, and 67).
☐   • a copy of form T2093, "Return of
Contributions to a Candidate at an Election
(National Revenue—Taxation)".
☐   (3) After 2 p.m. on nomination day, obtain from the
returning officer a list of the names of the
candidates nominated.

Sec. 26   If only one candidate has been officially
nominated, the returning officer is required to
declare him elected.

(c) PRELIMINARY LISTS OF ELECTORS
The procedure for enumeration, and the preparation
and revision of the preliminary lists of electors in
urban and rural polling divisions, are fully set out in
section 18 of the Act and in supporting schedules A
and B.

Sec. 18(12) ☐   (1) Receive copies of the printed preliminary lists
from the returning officer.

Sec. 28   ☐   (2) Inspect, in the office of the returning officer, the
lists of Canadian Forces and Public Service
electors prepared pursuant to the Special Voting
Rules.

Sec. 18   ☐   (3) Receive 5 copies of the Notice of Revision of the
Schedule A   urban lists of electors, from the returning officer.
Rule (34)   (4) Arrange to have representatives in attendance at:
Sec. 18   ☐   • *Each urban revisal office.* Two representatives
Schedule A   may, on the days specified on the Notice of
Rule (61)   Revision, attend, but may take part in the
proceedings only with the permission of the
revising officer.

Sec. 18   ☐   • *the place designated for revision by each rural
Schedule B   enumerator* in his Notice of Rural Enumeration.
Rules (3),   Only one representative may attend, between
(13),(14)   10 a.m. and 10 p.m. on Wednesday, the 19th day
before polling day. The representatives may take
part in the proceedings only with the permission
of the rural enumerator.

Sec. 18 ☐   (5) Receive 3 copies of the statement of changes and
Schedule A   additions to the preliminary lists from each urban
Rule (64)   revising officer.

Sec. 18(18) ☐   (6) Receive 1 copy of the statement of changes and
additions for each rural polling division from the
returning officer.

(d) THE POLL

The law governing an ordinary poll is contained in sections 33 to 51 of the Act. For an advance poll, see sections 91 to 97 of the Act.

(1) Receive from the returning officer:

Sec. 27(2) ☐   • 10 copies of the Notice of Grant of a Poll.

Sec. 92(3) ☐   • 5 copies of the Notice of Holding of Advance Poll.

Sec. 96(4) ☐   • a copy of each Record of Completed Affidavits for Voting at an Advance Poll.

Sec. 29(3) ☐   (2) Receive from the returning officer a list of the names and addresses of the deputy returning officers who will act at each polling station.

☐   (3) Using form 100, appoint persons to be agents of candidates at the polls.

Sec. 36
Sec. 37
Sec. 40(1)
Sec. 45(6)

     The primary function of the poll agents is to observe the proceedings at the polling station while voting is taking place, and during the counting of the votes. They have the right to require an elector to take a qualifying oath, *but have no right to question an elector.* Poll agents may examine a poll book during the hours that the poll is open, and may relay information from the poll book to any agent outside the polling station. Poll agents may enter and leave a polling station as they please during the hours that the poll is open, provided that no candidate has more than two agents present at one time.

Sec. 43(1,2) ☐   (4) Where necessary, instruct poll agents to obtain *transfer certificates* from the returning officer. Such a certificate will entitle a poll agent to vote at the polling station in which he is working—if that polling station is different from the one in which he would normally vote. To obtain a transfer certificate, the poll agent must present his appointment form, signed by the candidate, to the returning officer or the election clerk no later than 10 p.m. on the Friday before polling day.

Sec. 37(2)
Sec. 51(1)

☐ (5) Visit the polling stations on polling day. A candidate is entitled to act as his own agent at a polling station or assist his poll agents. The candidate and/or his poll agents may be present while voting is taking place, and during the addition of the votes on polling night.

(e) AFTER THE POLL

Sec. 53

The returning officer conducts the official addition of the votes. If fewer than 25 votes separate the two leading candidates, the returning officer must request a judicial recount. In the circumstances set out in subsection 56(1) of the Act, a candidate may himself apply to a judge for a recount.

Sec. 53(2)

☐ (1) Attend in person, or be represented at the official addition of the votes. The time and place are stated on the election Proclamation.

Sec. 53(6)

☐ (2) Receive, after the offical addition of the votes, a copy of the returning officer's certificate of the results of voting.

Sec. 56(1)

☐ (3) In the circumstances set out in subsection 56(1) of the Act, apply for a judicial recount.

(4) If a recount is ordered:

Sec. 56(4,6)

☐ • attend in person, or send representatives. The time and place is stated in the judge's notice.

Sec. 56(18)(b)

☐ • receive from the judge a certificate of the results of his recount.

Sec. 58(4)

☐ (5) Receive a copy of the return to the writ from the returning officer. This is the *official declaration* that a candidate is elected. Note the date on the form—this is the date from which the time limits for various financial obligations run.

Sec. 59

☐ (6) Submit in writing to the Chief Electoral Officer any complaints or suggestions with respect to the election, the *Canada Elections Act*, or the conduct of an election officer. The Chief

Electoral Officer is required to include such a statement in his report to the Speaker of the House of Commons.

Sec. 62(17,18) (7) Give a statement of personal expenses to his
☐   official agent within one month after the candidate returned has been officially declared
Sec. 2   elected.
"Personal   "Personal expenses" is defined in section 2 of the
expenses"   Act. The amount must not exceed $2,000.

Sec. 63(1,2) ☐ (8) Have the candidate's "Return Respecting Election Expenses" completed. For further details, refer to Part A:3(a) of this Manual.

Sec. 63(1) ☐ (9) Have the "Candidate's Return Respecting Election Expenses" sent to the returning officer no later than two months after the candidate returned has been officially declared elected. Subsections 63(8) to 63(18) of the Act set out the legal consequences of not filing a return or declaration, or making a false statement.

Sec. 63(6) ☐ (10) Pay the returning officer the cost of publishing the summary of the return in a local newspaper.

Sec. 63(3) ☐ (11) Submit a candidate's declaration respecting election expenses (form no. 66 or 67) to the returning officer, within ten weeks after the candidate returned has been officially declared elected. This declaration must be made before the returning officer, a notary public, or a justice of the peace.

Sec. 63(4,5) ☐ (12) If necessary, submit a supplementary return for any late payments of accounts, or if contributions are received too late to be included in the initial return. This situation may arise if a bill is delayed by the death of a creditor, or if a judge has ordered payment of an account.

This "Candidate's Diary" is taken from the *Manual of Information Respecting Candidates*, by the kind permission of Mr. Jean-Marc Hamel, Chief Electoral Officer of Canada.

Bibliography

Aitken, Margaret. *Hey, Ma! I Did It.* Clarke Irwin, Toronto, 1953.

Bailey, Robert. *Radicals in Urban Politics.* University of Chicago Press, Chicago and London, 1974.

Baus, Herbert M., and William B. Ross. *Politics Battle Plan.* Macmillan, New York, 1968.

Bernays, Edward L., ed. *The Engineering of Consent.* University of Oklahoma Press, Norman, Oklahoma, 1955.

Bogart, Leon. *Silent Politics.* Wiley-Interscience, Toronto, 1972.

Bruno, Jerry, and Jeff Greenfield. *The Advance Man.* Morrow, New York, 1971.

Bullitt, Stimson. *To Be a Politician.* Yale University Press, New Haven, Conn., 1977.

Canada Elections Act. Statutes of Canada, Chapter 14, 1974. Queen's Printer, Ottawa. (With index.)

Canadian Advertising Rates and Data. Published monthly. 481 University Avenue, Toronto.

Cannon, James M. *Politics, U.S.A.* Doubleday, Toronto, 1960.

Cantril, Hadley. *Gauging Public Opinion.* Princeton University Press, Princeton, N.J., 1947.

Crouse, Timothy. *The Boys on the Bus.* Random House, New York, 1973.

Denman, Norris. *How To Organize an Election.* Les Editions du Jour, Montreal, 1962.

Erdos, Paul L. *Professional Mail Surveys*. McGraw-Hill, New York, 1970.

Fenton, John M. *In Your Opinion*. Little, Brown and Company, Boston, 1960.

Furhammar, Leif, and Folke Isaksson. *Politics and Film*. Translated by Kersti French. Praeger, New York, 1971.

Herzberg, Donald G., and J. W. Peltason. *A Student Guide to Campaign Politics*. McGraw-Hill Paperbacks, Toronto, 1970.

How To Win. Edited for the AFL-CIO Committee on Political Education, Washington, D.C., 1960.

Ingman, Dan. *Television Advertising*. Business Publications Ltd., London, England, 1965.

Instructions for Returning Officers. Chief Electoral Officer, Ottawa, Ontario, 1970.

Kelley, Stanley. *Professional Public Relations and Political Power*. The Johns Hopkins Press, Baltimore, 1956.

Lash, Joseph P. *Eleanor and Franklin*. Norton, New York, 1971.

Leuthold, David A. *Electioneering in a Democracy*. Wiley, New York, 1968.

Luck, David J., et al. *Marketing Research*. Prentice-Hall, Englewood, N.J., 1974.

Manual of Information Respecting Candidates, Official Agents, and Auditors. Published by the Chief Electoral Officer, 440 Coventry Road, Ottawa, Ontario, K1A 0M6, 1977.

Massie, Robert K. *Nicholas and Alexandra*. Atheneum, New York, 1967.

Masson, J., and J. Anderson, eds. *Emerging Party Politics in Urban Canada*. University of Alberta, Edmonton, 1972.

May, Ernest R., and Janet Fraser, eds. *Campaign '72*. Harvard University Press, Cambridge, Mass., 1973.

Meyer, P. Swing. *The Winning Candidate*. H. H. Heineman, New York, 1966.

Morrison, Herbert. *Government and Parliament*. Oxford University Press, Toronto, 1954.

Murphy, William T., Jr., and Edward Schneier. *Vote Power*. Anchor-Doubleday, New York, 1974.

Nimmo, Dan. *The Policy Persuaders*. Prentice-Hall, New York, 1970.

Paltiel, K. Z. *Political Party Financing in Canada*. McGraw-Hill, Toronto, 1970.

Parkinson, Hank. *Winning Your Campaign: A Nuts-and-Bolts Guide to Political Victory*. Prentice-Hall, New York, 1970.

Patterson, Thomas E., and Robert D. McClure. *The Unseeing Eye*. Putnam, New York, 1976.

Perry, James M. *The New Politics*. Potter, New York, 1968.

Polsby, Nelson W., and Aaron B. Wildarsky. *Presidential Elections*. 3rd ed. Charles Scribner's Sons, New York, 1971.

Provincial Elections Act, Revised Statutes of British Columbia, 1960, Chapter 306, as amended. Queen's Printer, Victoria, 1975. (With index.)

Qualter, T. H. *The Election Process in Canada*. McGraw-Hill, Toronto, 1970.

Roll, Jr., Charles W., and Albert H. Cantril. *Polls: Their Use and Misuse in Politics*. Basic Books, New York, 1972.

Rose, Richard. *Influencing Voters*. Faber and Faber, London, 1967.

Royko, Mike. *Boss: Richard J. Daley of Chicago*. New American Library, Scarborough, Ontario, 1971.

Scammon, Richard M., and Ben J. Wattenberg. *The Real Majority*. Coward-McCann, New York, 1970.

Shadegg, Stephen C. *How To Win an Election*. Taplinger Publishing, New York, 1964.

Sherman, Paddy. *Bennett*. McClelland and Stewart, Toronto, 1966.

Simpson, Dick W. *Winning Elections: A Handbook in Participatory Politics*. Swallow Press, Chicago, 1972.

Stavis, Ben. *We Were the Campaign*. Beacon Press, Boston, 1969.

Steinberg, Arnold. *Political Campaign Management, A Systems Approach*. Lexington Books, Lexington, Mass., 1976.

Thompson, Hunter S. *Fear and Loathing on the Campaign Trail '72*. Straight Arrow Books, San Francisco, 1973.

Tooke, Moyra. *Politics Are People*. Griffin House, Toronto, 1974.

Van Riper, Paul P. *Handbook of Practical Politics*. Harper and Row, New York, 1967.

Walzer, Michael. *Political Action*. Quadrangle Books, Chicago, 1971.

Webb, Kenneth, and Harry P. Hatry. *Obtaining Citizen Feedback*. The Urban Institute, Washington, D.C., 1973.

Weingast, David E. *We Elect a President*. Julian Messner, New York, 1964.

White, Theodore H. *The Making of the President 1960*. Atheneum, New York, 1961 (and subsequent editions 1964, 1968, 1972).

Witcove, Jules. *Marathon: The Pursuit of the Presidency, 1972-76*. Signet, Scarborough, Ontario, 1978.

Wyckoff, Gene. *The Image Candidates: American Politics in the Age of Television*. Macmillan, New York, 1968.